On the Trail

LAURA MARSH

ISBN: 1505291046
ISBN-13: 978-1505291049

DEDICATION

First of all, I want to thank God for the inspiration and words to write this book.

I want to thank John, my "Baby," for helping me to see what I needed to see.

To Brother Dave, St. Benedict the Moor, St. James, St. John's Cathedral, and all of the other meal sites; please keep doing what you are doing. You are saving lives every day.

Thank you so much for your love and support. To my mom, my daughter, Cynthia, and the rest of my family, I'm sorry that it took me so long to get it right. I love you a 'circle's worth'!

Last, but not least, I want to say thank you to my homeless family. Keep God in your hearts and always remember that you are special.

CONTENTS

ACKNOWLEDGMENTS

John and I always acknowledge God first.
Without Him we are nothing.

I want to thank John for always being there for me; good or bad.
I love you.

Arn and Norma Quakkelaar helped us publish our first book.
They took me off the streets and let me live with them for a whole
year while John recovered from a gunshot wound to the face.
Their unconditional love literally gave us our lives back.
I know they saved me. We love you!

We want to thank our new friend Heather for working so hard on
our behalf without expecting a thing. I don't know how we would
have published our second book without you.
You are such a generous woman. Thank you!

To my beautiful daughter, Cynthia Marie Ramos,
I love you more than one hundred whole skies!
(As you used to say when you were little.)

I can't forget my homeless family. We have a bond with you guys
that none of these people will ever understand. Keep your heads
up. "Freedom Fighter" still fights the good fight! We love you!

AUTHOR'S NOTE

John and I met at St. Ben's church eight and a half years ago. We were both homeless and looking forward to St. Ben's evening meal. When he first looked at me I felt like I was struck by lightning. It was love from then on. Our lives on the streets had me down until John started urging me to write about our struggle. He helped me look at everything differently. I wrote like crazy!

When John was shot in the face during a robbery, my whole world ended. He was my protector on the streets. What was I to do?

Well, God sent Arn and Norma to save my life. They took me in for a whole year while John healed in the hospital.

Our dream is to open up houses or a building for the homeless. We need to save these people. After all, we are all God's children!

1 PERSONALITIES

There is a pretty decent sized group of deaf people who are camping out. I find it very interesting to watch them interact with each other. They sign when they are together, but they read our lips as we talk to them. They are very outgoing and never seem to have any trouble with anyone else. I am just glad to call them family!

There is a man that I call "70-Cent Man." Every time we are all putting together to buy something, he only has seventy cents. No more, no less!

There is an older black man that I refer to as the "'70s Man." He wears seventies clothes and sports a big afro. He reminds me of what a Black Panther would look like. I want to throw up a fist and yell, "Power to the people!" when I see him! On the serious side, he is a really nice man.

There is a group of young people who hang out together. They usually have some sort of drama going on. One day somebody in the group got some money. They all came in wearing new outfits and the ladies all had their hair done. They burst into St Ben's dramatically and stood there for special effect. After they were seen by everyone, they got in line to get their trays. (I guess they spent so much on hair and clothes that they couldn't afford restaurant food!). I call them "The Entourage."

As I sit here at the St. Ben's table, I look around. Children are running to and fro. They are playing with the different homeless guests. As I watch this I'm struck again with the intense feeling of "family" in the room. These children have no fear whatsoever of the people here. Yet adult strangers turn their heads in fear when they see the same people. Isn't it amazing that we could learn so much from children? Is it making you look at yourself right now?

There is a young man that I will refer to as "T". He is a basically a good guy. I don't know a lot about his story. I do know that I worry about him. He has had many brain surgeries and he has seizures. He still tries to work through temporary services. I believe he wants better for his life. He does stay in a bit of drama with certain other people, but he gets along with people for the most part. I wish I knew more to tell you about him.

Single women

As I walk past the meal site tables, I look around at everybody. I see a lot of couples. While most couples don't make it out here, there are quite a few who have weathered the storm. We women go through so much on the street. As single women, we are often beaten and raped, only to see the same man saunter into the meal site the next day. He is so confident that we won't tell that he doesn't bother to hide. So, we run to a man for protection. We look for love and safety. What we usually find is a man who is mentally and physically abusive. We live in fear daily. We walk around with our bruises. We often lie about where they came from because we are embarrassed, but everybody knows where they came from. They know her man is beating her.

I was that woman more than once.

If the couple is suffering from drug and alcohol addiction, the man may prostitute the woman out to support their habit. This doesn't happen in every case, but does happen quite frequently. As long as she is making enough money things are good between them. She is always taking a chance with her life every time she gets in the car with a stranger. She may get beaten or raped a few times. But she will continue on to feed her and her man's addiction. Once she stops making money for him he will probably beat her up and leave her alone in the streets. If she goes to jail he will probably move on.

I don't look down on any woman in that situation, because I was that woman more than once.

Mishka

In the first book I briefly mentioned a woman who speaks six or seven languages. I also mentioned that she and I were always at odds, yet we would always help each other.

When she disappeared from the downtown area, I didn't think much of it. She's not taking her psych meds and she's on drugs pretty bad. Every time I see her, she looks worse. She would constantly pick fights with everyone. I could tell that she was losing it. I felt bad for her. She can speak all of these languages yet her mental illness took over. As with many other mentally ill people she was self-medicating with drugs. We haven't seen her in six months.

Today I was sitting in my car at St. Ben's and she came up to my window. She looked so healthy! Her speech was normal and she was making sense. She gave me a hug through the window. I've never seen her look so good! She looked at me and said, "I think I'll stay on my medication." She told me that she'd been in jail for six months, so that means she's been on her meds for six months. I was happy for her. Then comes the usual bad news. She told me that the shelter was full and she had nowhere to go. I wanted to take her home with me, but we already had a bunch of people in our small apartment. She told me that she was thinking of sleeping in a dope house, but also told me that she didn't want to start using again. I was heartbroken. It's almost like single women are set up to fail on the streets. I told her about a nice shelter in Waukesha. I don't know if she ever went there.

It's been almost a year since I've seen Mishka. I don't know what happened to her. All I can do is pray that she is clean and happy. God bless you, Miss Alicia.

This is an update: It's been two years since we've seen Mishka. Our prayers continue to be with her

2 JAZZ IN THE PARK

We have enjoyed Jazz in the Park every week in the summer since we were homeless. So, today we were planning on going. John and I got up super early to run all of our errands. We like to take some food and a cooler full of ice-cold sodas. We were trying to figure out what we could make for everybody. We needed enough to go around.

We were discussing this at my psychiatrist appointment. I saw the psych doctor. John and I were on our way out when Jenna stopped us. Let me show you how good God is! She said, "We have a lot of food left over from our party. Do you know someone who could use it?" A light bulb went off! We could feed our homeless family at Jazz in the Park! John was telling me that nobody was going to eat it.

We loaded the food up in the car. We went to the store for sodas and ice for the cooler. We arrived at Jazz in the Park. A large group of homeless men carried the food and cooler to a table in the park. I was hoping that a few people would eat.

A group of twenty to twenty five homeless people gathered around the table. We prayed. We learned that many of these people are barred from the meal sites and would have otherwise gone hungry. For many, this was their only meal for the day. When they left the table, the food was almost completely gone. We opened up the cooler and passed out cold grape sodas. Everyone was grateful. The atmosphere was one of "family."

We were all talking when the police showed up. The "Homeless

Table" is always a table of interest for the police at concerts. The police always watch us so they can catch us with a beer can. Apparently, generic grape soda cans resemble Milwaukee's Best beer cans!

They thought they caught us that time!

3 RIVER RHYTHMS

Today was such a beautiful day! We went to River Rhythms at Pere Marquette Park. There is a free band, a beer tent, a hot food tent, and a popcorn maker. People bring their folding chairs. The homeless people mingle with the upper-class. Most of us don't look like we are homeless. So, they smile and talk to us.

I remember going there two years before John got shot. We would all meet up at River Rhythms. As we mingled with the upper-class we actually became friends with them. I remember the prettiest little blue-eyed girl named Olive. She was so outgoing! She happily played with children of all races. You could tell right away what a wonderful family she came from. John and I had a chance to meet her sister and parents. They had a warm smile and even warmer eyes. I felt that these people were non-judgmental. I confided in Olive's parents about our homelessness. They had many questions, which I happily answered. I told them about the book I was writing. They were very encouraging.

So, we would see them every week at River Rhythms.

After not seeing them for two years we decided to go to River Rhythms. We had been there a few times. I found myself looking for them. I didn't see them anywhere. I was looking for Olive.

I was sitting at a table looking around for them. I spied a little girl, with blond hair, running through the crowd. The only way to be sure it was Olive was to see her parents. I let my eyes follow her progress through the crowd. I was excited to see that it was them!

I started heading towards them. I wasn't sure if they would remember me. As I approached them, I saw the look of recognition on their faces. Their warm smiles were once again upon us. Olive's mother commented that she had wondered about us and the book over the years. I told her about the first book getting published. We shared with them about John getting shot. They were so happy to see how good he was doing. We were so excited to tell them that we had given our lives to God. I told them how they had touched our lives. It was a great conversation! We look forward to seeing them every summer!

The Food Tent

A few years ago we befriended the couple who runs the food tent at River Rhythms. Their names are Mary and John. They would take whatever food they didn't sell and give it to us homeless people. John and Mary probably didn't even realize how they touched our lives with that one simple gesture every week. Some people are barred from the dinner meal site. Therefore, they are pretty hungry. They were grateful for the unexpected meal.

We were at River Rhythms, as usual. I walked over to the food tent and got in line. I was hoping that they remembered us. When it was my turn, I stepped up to John and Mary. Mary's eyes got big and her smile got even bigger! She was genuinely happy to see me. I told them that I wasn't sure if they would remember me. She said, "We would never forget you guys!" I was about to cry! I told them about how good we are doing. I also told them about John getting shot. At that point I went to find John.

I found John and told him that I wanted to show him something. We walked up to the food tent. John and Mary were happy to see how good John was doing. We all talked for awhile. They offered us something to eat. We declined. We are blessed to have plenty of food at home. We were so touched that they offered us something to eat that I was about to cry again! Mary gave me a hug over her row of pans. It was so touching!

Now I only had to find the lady with the little white dog!

Connie and Doody

John and I were at River Rhythms sitting with our homeless family. I was looking around at everyone and spied a little white dog. I knew at once that it was Doody! I looked at his owner. It was Connie! In the first book I talked about a nice woman who would see us at the park. She would sit down with us and talk. She even bought an unfinished book from us. Connie knew about us being homeless, but it didn't bother her in the least. She asked questions. She was honest and straight forward. We really liked her a lot. We always looked forward to seeing her. She was so kind. She had touched our lives in a very special way! Praise God!

When I approached Connie I was so glad that she remembered us! I said, "Excuse me, ma'am, does this dog go by the name Doody?" She said, "Why yes he does!" Her smile was very welcoming. It was such a treat that John and I got to see all of these people who had touched our lives while on the street. I know there are more homeless people with similar stories about someone who touched them. To the people who are like these previously mentioned, thank you so much for caring about those less fortunate. You are beautiful people.

.

4 INTERVIEWS WITH THE HOMELESS

Donald...

1. How long have you been homeless?
[question not asked in this interview]

2. What circumstances led you to be homeless?
I lost my job.

3. Where do you sleep at night?
I sleep in the courtyard behind the courthouse and county jail.

4 Do you get harassed by the police?
No, I don't get harassed by the police.

5. How do you feel about Milwaukee shelters?
I can't stand the shelters in Milwaukee.

6. Do you think there's enough help out here for us?
Yes, I guess there is enough help.

7. What is the hardest part of being homeless?
Finding somewhere to sleep is the hardest part of being homeless.

8. What is the main thing holding you back?
   I'm the main thing holding myself back.

9. How far did you go in school?
   I went as far as the eighth grade.

10. Do you have any job skills?
    Yes, I do home improvement.

11. How easy/hard is it to get a job?
    It's hard as hell to get a job!

12. If someone were to offer you a chance to make it off the streets, would you be willing to work hard?
    Yeah, I would work hard.

13. Do you have a chronic illness?
    No, I am very healthy.

14. Do you suffer from mental illness?
    Yes, I do.

15. Does mental illness run in your family?
    Yes, mental illness runs on my mother's side of the family.

16. Do you have adequate health insurance?
    No, I do not have adequate health insurance.

17. How do the streets affect you mentally?
    The secret is getting enough sleep. I get a little crazy when I don't get enough rest.

18. Do you have addictions? Would you please share what kind?
    I smoke marijuana and cigarettes.

19. What was your childhood like?
    My childhood was pretty good.

20. Are you on good terms with your family?
    Yes, I am.

21. What makes you special?
I have a great sense of humor.

Is there something else that you would like people to know about being homeless?
I can tell you one thing about homelessness. It will chew you up and spit you out.

———————

Brian...

1. How long have you been homeless?
I have been homeless on and off for ten years.

2. What circumstances led you to be homeless?
I've been using drugs and alcohol. Drinking is my main problem.

2. Where do you sleep at night?
I am staying with a friend right now. I get food stamps, so I buy food to pay my way.

3. Do you get harassed by the police?
I don't get harassed by the police anymore. They used to be real bad about that.

4 How do you feel about Milwaukee shelters?
I feel good about the shelters.

5. Do you think there's enough help out here for us?
Yes, there most definitely is enough help.

6. What is the hardest part of being homeless?
The weather is the hardest part of being homeless. You have to get a good spot in bad weather like rain or snow.

7. What is the main thing holding you back?
I'm depressed right now and I've been drinking. I try to go to the temporary services, but they are so far away. I might not have

bus fare and I'll walk way out there. Then, they send out everyone else first. So, I probably won't get sent out.

8. How far did you go in school?
I graduated high school.

9. Do you have any job skills?
I was a cook from the ages of eighteen to thirty four years old. I always worked in fancy restaurants. It's very stressful.

10. How easy/hard is it to get a job?
Like I said, the temporary services are no guarantee that I will work. Other people get sent out first. The temp services are far away and I may not have bus fare.

11. If someone were to offer you a chance to make it off the streets would you be willing to work hard?
Of course I would work hard (but not in a restaurant!).

12. Do you have a chronic illness?
No, I am very healthy.

13. Do you suffer from mental illness?
No, I do not.

14. Does mental illness run in your family?
No, it doesn't.

15. Do you have adequate health insurance?
My health insurance is okay. I haven't had to see a doctor in over ten years.

16. How do the streets affect you mentally?
Being on the streets doesn't really affect me. It's a peace of mind. There's no stress.

17. Do you have addictions?
I drink alcohol and smoke weed. I haven't smoked crack for over five years.

18. What was your childhood like?

My childhood was excellent. I was raised in a good environment.

19. Are you on good terms with your family?

Yes, I am. I occasionally rent a room from my sister. When I want to be by myself I come back out here.

20. What makes you special?

I can make you a great meal!

Is there something else that you would like people to know about being homeless?

If you live on the street, stay to yourself. Don't hang out with people. They screw you over every time. If they think they can get you they will rob you.

Barbara...

1. How long have you been homeless?

4 years

2. What circumstances lead you to be homeless?

I suffered from depression, I wasn't working, and I was in an abusive relationship.

3. Where do you sleep at night?

I sleep here and there, basically wherever I can.

4. Do you get harassed by the police?

Yes, they know me by name.

5. How do you feel about Milwaukee shelters?

They are good for men, but not for single women.

6. Do you think there's enough help out here for us?

There is help out here, but resources aren't advertised. We all go by word-of-mouth.

7. What is the hardest part of being homeless?
People's perception of the homeless is typical stereotyping. We are all out here for different reasons.

8. What is the main thing holding you back?
My self-esteem is so low. I suffer from depression.

9. How far did you go in school?
I had 2 years of college.

10. Do you have any job skills?
Yes, I have plenty.

11. How easy/hard is it to find a job out here?
It's easy to get a temporary job.

12. If someone were to give you a chance to make it off the street, would you be willing to work hard?
Of course I would work hard!

13. Do you have a chronic illness?
I have high blood pressure..

14. Do you suffer from mental illness?
Yes, as I've said before, I suffer from depression.

15. Does mental illness run in your family?
No, mental illness does not run in my family.

16. Do you have adequate healthcare?
I have been on a waiting list to renew my insurance for over a year.

17. How do the streets affect you mentally?
I am definitely crazier!

18. Do you have addictions?
Yes, alcohol.

19. What was your childhood like?
I had a loving single mother. There was nothing bad.

20. Are you on good terms with your family?
Yes.

21. What makes you special?
I see the bright side of people. I try to become a better person every day.

———————

Kathy...

1. How long have you been homeless?
[question not asked in this interview]

2. What circumstances led you to be homeless?
The office manager kicked me out because I was not on the lease.

3. Where do you sleep at night?
I stay at the single women's shelter.

4. Do you get harassed by the police?
No. Sometimes, they take me out to mental health.

5 How do you feel about Milwaukee shelters?
We are blessed to have the shelters.

6. Do you think there's enough help out here for us?
Hell no! Can we get a phone to use?

7. What is the hardest part of being homeless?
We are not guaranteed to eat. We are overburdened with bag and baggage. We can't take care of our health or hygiene properly.

8. What is the main thing holding you back?
I'm waiting for a bed. I have no loving friends or family to turn to.

9. How far did you go in school?
   I went as far as eighth grade.

10. Do you have any job skills?
    Yes, I've worked in food service.

11. How easy/hard is it to get a job?
    Getting a job is a 50/50 chance. If you do get a job while on the streets, you have to worry about a clean uniform, how you will travel, are you on call, etc...

12. If someone gave you a chance to make it off the streets, would you be willing to work hard?
    Yes, as long as they don't touch my money or medications!

13. Do you have a chronic illness?
    Yes, I have breathing problems and Edema.

14. Do you suffer from mental illness?
    Yes.

15. Does mental illness run in your family?
    Yes.

16. Do you have adequate health insurance?
    Yes.

17. How do the streets affect you mentally?
    I am too old and have given too much to be out here.

18. Do you have addictions?
    If you consider legal drugs such as pain pills and cigarettes.

19. What was your childhood like?
    [No answer.]

20. Are you on good terms with your family?
    Hell, no! They are abusive and won't help financially.

21. What makes you special?
    I give my all to cleanliness and neatness.

_____

Ann…

1. How long have you been homeless?
   This time around is one year.

2. What circumstances led you to be homeless?
   The building that I was living in was sold.

3. Where do you sleep at night?
   I sleep on the heater vent outside.

4. Do you ever get harassed by the police?
   Sometimes I do. About 25% of them are nice. The other 75% are not nice.

5. How do you feel about Milwaukee shelters?
   They're full of it!

6. Do you think there's enough help out here for us?
   No!

7. What is the hardest part of being homeless?
   I am a woman in unsafe surroundings, who is subject to rape at any given time. I don't get any sleep.

8. What is the main thing holding you back?
   I'm having a hard time finding the right payee who won't steal from me.

9. How far did you go in school?
   10th grade

10. Do you have any job skills?
    I've worked in sales, deli prep, and childcare.

11. How easy/hard is it to get a job?

It's very hard to get a job out here. SSI needs to let us handle our own money! Payees and agencies are always taking our money!

12. If someone gave you a chance to make it off the streets, would you be willing to work hard?

Yes

13. Do you have a chronic illness?

Yes, sleep apnea.

14. Do you suffer from mental illness?

Yes, I have depression.

15. Does mental illness run in your family?

Not really.

16. Do you have adequate health insurance?

No, I don't.

17. How do the streets affect you mentally?

The streets drain me mentally and emotionally.

18. Do you have addictions?

I only smoke cigarettes.

19. What was your childhood like?

It was horrible!

20. Are you on good terms with your family?

No, I am not!

21. What makes you special?

I am a very good-hearted person. I am always getting taken advantage of. I need some more support.

———————

Steven...

1. How long have you been homeless?
[question not asked in this interview]

2. What circumstances led you to be homeless?
It was a lack of communication with the landlord and the people that I was staying with.

3. Where do you sleep at night?
I sleep in the streets or wherever available. I don't sleep in structures or buildings. I stick to open areas.

4. Do you get harassed by the police?
Not lately. They don't bother me much.

5. How do you feel about Milwaukee shelters?
Rules are fair. Some people who work there are selfish. They pick favorite homeless people who get special treatment.

6. Do you think there is enough help out here for us?
No, there aren't enough shelters out here for everyone.

7. What is the hardest part of being homeless?
Weather conditions are the hardest thing to deal with.

8. What is the main thing holding you back?
Myself.

9. How far did you go in school?
I went as far as 12th grade and got kicked out. Then, I got my G.E.D.

10. Do you have any job skills?
I've worked in a foundry, did carpentry, moving, manufacturing, landscaping, etc.

11. How easy/hard is it to get a job?
There's an 85% chance that you won't get a job. The other 15% is if you know someone.

12. If someone were to offer you a chance to get off the street would you be willing to work
   Yes, I would!

13. Do you have a chronic illness?
   No.

14. Do you suffer from mental illness?
   [No answer.]

15. Does mental illness run in your family?
   No.

16. Do you have adequate health insurance?
   No.

17. How do the streets affect you mentally?
   It's all about survival and dealing with many different personalities. Even our surroundings are different every day. You have to adapt to any situation and keep an open mind 24 hours a day.

18. Do you have addictions? If yes, would you be able to share what kind?
   Yes, marijuana and cigarettes.

19. What was your childhood like?
   It was very good.

20. Are you on good terms with your family?
   Yes, excellent terms.

21. What makes you special?
   I believe in Lord God. That's what makes me different. I'm a believer.

Tercell...

1. How long have you been homeless?
   I have been homeless for two years.

2. What circumstances led you to be homeless?
   I suffered a loss of income.

3. Where do you sleep at night?
   I sleep in the woods.

4. Do you get harassed by the police?
   Yes, I do.

5. How do you feel about Milwaukee shelters?
   I hate them.

6. Do you think there is enough help out here for us?
   No, there's not enough help.

7. What is the hardest part of being homeless?
   The hardest part of being homeless is finding a place to sleep.

8. What is the main thing holding you back?
   Family is the main thing holding me back.

9. How far did you go in school?
   I went through the twelfth grade and I graduated.

10. Do you have any job skills?
    Yes, I do.

11. How easy/hard is it to get a job?
    It's very hard to get a job.

12. If someone were to offer you a chance to make it off the street, would you be willing to work hard?
    Yes, I would.

13. Do you have a chronic illness?
    [No answer.]

14. Do you suffer from mental illness?
    Yes, I do.

15. Does mental illness run in your family?
    Yes, it does.

16. Do you have adequate health insurance?
    No, I don't.

17. How do the streets affect you mentally?
    The streets affect you very badly.

18. Do you have any addictions? Will you share what kind?
    I have no addictions.

19. What was your childhood like?
    My childhood was good.

20. Are you on good terms with your family?
    No, I am not on good terms with my family.

21. What makes you special?
    I am very intelligent!

———————

5 HOMELESS SUCCESS STORIES

Anonymous Success Story #1…

1. How long were you homeless?
   I was homeless for ten years.

2. Where did you sleep at?
   I slept outside at the park.

3. How did being homeless affect you mentally?
   I am mentally ill.

4. Did you feel like people looked down on you?
   Yes, I did.

5. Are you chronically physically or mentally ill?
   I am mentally ill.

6. How was your childhood?
   It was good.

7. Do you feel like there's enough help out here for homeless people?
   Nope, naw, no way!

8. Do you have any job skills or did you complete college?
   Yes, I have job skills and I also went to college for awhile.

9. Do you have any family or friends who will help you?
   I don't know.

10. How were you able to get off the streets?
    I got help through a community shelter.

Anything else you want to add?
   Being homeless will totally stress you out. It's so bad that nobody wants to have anything to do with me.

———————————

Anonymous Success Story #2...

1. How long were you homeless?
   I was homeless for six years.

2. Where did you sleep at?
   I slept anywhere safe.

3. How did being homeless affect you mentally?
   It kept me up and down in my feelings.

4. Did you feel like people looked down on you?
   No, I didn't.

5. Are you chronically physically or mentally ill?
   No, I am not.

6. How was your childhood?
   It was happy and safe.

7. Do you feel like there is enough help for homeless people?
   No, but they are trying.

8. Do you have any job skills or did you complete college?
   Yes, I went to trade school.

9. Do you have any family or friends who would help you?
    Yes, out of town. But I've already been helped.

10. How were you able to make it off the streets?
    Community Advocates helped me get off the street.

Interview conducted by Stephen A. Polk

Anonymous Success Story #3...

1. How long were you homeless?
   I was homeless for about a year.

2. Where did you sleep at?
   I slept in an abandoned house.

3. How did being homeless affect you mentally?
   It affected me really badly.

4. Did you feel like people looked down on you?
   No, I didn't.

5. Are you chronically mentally or physically ill?
   Yes, I suffer from both.

6. How was your childhood?
   It was okay.

7. Do you feel like there's enough help out here for homeless people?
   Yes, I do.

8. Do you have any job skills or did you complete college?
   No, but I am going to school right now.

9. Do you have any friends or family who will help you?
   No.

10. How were you able to get off the streets?
I had an income so I looked for an apartment.

Anything else you would like to add?
Homeless people need to have more access to jobs.

———————

Dennis…

1. How long were you homeless?
I was homeless for five years.

2. Where did you sleep at?
I slept everywhere and anywhere I could lay my head.

3. How did being homeless affect you mentally?
It fucked me up.

4. Did you feel like people looked down on you?
Hell yeah!

5. Are you chronically or physically ill?
Hell yeah I am!

6. How was your childhood?
It was good.

7. Do you feel like there is enough help for homeless people?
Hell, no there isn't enough help!

8. Do you have any job skills or did you complete college?
No I don't

9. Do you have any friends or family who will help you?
Yes, I do.

10. How were you able to get off the streets?
I was able to get off the streets by the strength of God. If it had been left up to me I'd still be on the streets.

Anything else you would like to add?
If you got God in your life you'll make it.

Deanna...

1. How long were you homeless?
I was homeless for a total of three years. Not all of them were here in Milwaukee.

2. Where did you sleep at?
I've slept several places. I slept in apartment building hallways, storefront doorways. I slept anyplace I could lay my head.

3. How did being homeless affect you mentally?
It put my life into perspective.

4. Did you feel like people looked down on you?
I remember walking in the downtown area, and two professional people walked past me. The lady said, (as she moved over), "I don't like street people!"

5. Are you chronically physically or mentally ill?
No.

6. How was your childhood?
It was normal until the age of 12.

7. Do you feel like there is enough help for the homeless?
Yes, but homeless people don't take advantage of the resources!

8. Do you have any job skills or did you complete college?
I did complete college.

9. Do you have any friends or family who would help you?
No!

10. How were you able to get off the street?
I found that the streets weren't for me. Some people can make

it, some people can't.

Anything else you would like to add?
If you see homeless people on the street don't ignore them or talk about them. (Help them!) Say hi, how are you today?

Anonymous Success Story #4...

1. How long were you homeless?
I was homeless for four years.

2. Where did you sleep at?
I used to sleep under the bridge.

3. How did being homeless affect you mentally?
Being homeless made me not trust anyone anymore. The homeless steal from the homeless. Who can you trust?

4. Did you feel like people looked down on you?
Some people looked down on me, but not all of them. Some helped me more than others.

5. Are you chronically physically or mentally ill?
I suffer from both, but not chronically. I have pain here and there.

6. How was your childhood?
My childhood was not the best in the world. I was tortured by step parents and step siblings.

7. Do you feel like there's enough help for homeless people?
No, there could be more meal sites and shelters and they shouldn't be run by assholes. We have to be broke to stay at the men's shelter. It used to be that you could go there with an income and they would put your money up for you until you move. Now, if they find out that you have money they kick you out. Don't get me started on this subject!

8. Do you have any job skills or did you complete college?
   I went to school for culinary. I have been a body guard, also.

9. Do you have any family or friends who will help you?
   I have one family member who will help me. The other one is too far away.

10. How were you able to get off the streets?
    Red Cross put me in a program and helped me get my benefits.

Anything else you would like to add?
   People look down on the homeless. We can't afford to get where rich people are. What if they become homeless? Nobody is going to help them. They won't have a home. What are they going to do? They won't make it out here.

---

6 I GO BACK…

I go back…
> And see all of the familiar faces. Why are they still out here years later?

I go back…
> And see that the police are still abusing and harassing the homeless people. Aren't our lives hard enough?

I go back…
> And it's all about getting drunk on the trail. Some things never change!

I go back…
> And people still stereotype us. Don't they know that we are human, too?

I go back…
> And find that many of my beloved family members have died. Will they be in heaven when I get there?

I go back…
> And relive all of the memories of my time on the streets. It was definitely a humbling experience.

I go back...

> And thank God Almighty that I survived to see yet another glorious day!!

7 DON'T WANT TO LEAVE

John and I have been off the streets for over two years. John always gets up early. He prays and then he hops up. He's very chipper! (And very annoying if you ask me!) He immediately asks me, "What all do we have to do today?" I don't even open my eyes. I just ask, "Where's the coffee?" John hasn't been able to drive since he got shot, so I do the all of the driving. The reason I say all this is because John will never be able to drive again due to seizures resulting from the gunshot. We always have an appointment or somewhere to go.

The issue that I am having is that every time I leave, I can't wait to get back home! I have absolutely no desire to leave the safety of my house. I have lived a very of dangerous life on the streets for a long time. I feel that I have no business hanging out in the streets, unless I am visiting our family members. I feel bad that so many people are sleeping outside. I just want to take everyone home with us!

This is how the next story starts...

John and I have big dreams of opening some homes or a shelter for the homeless. We don't want to stop at just providing shelter. We want to deal with the person's full needs, including mental and physical, job skills, or whatever else is needed to help the person be independent again. We have been waiting for God's direction. While we have been waiting, we have been busy!

When John first came home from the nursing home, we were able to rent a two bedroom apartment. It wasn't the nicest place to live, but it was ours. The landlord knew that we often had people staying with us. He just asked to see each person's identification so he would know who was in the building. Ever since John came home, we have had various homeless people stay with us. At first, we took a couple of "long-timers" home with us. These are people who we have known for over ten years. We have seen each other at our lowest point. We usually know who we can trust (although some people will unexpectedly rip us off).

So, we let couples use the other bedroom. Then, we had a person on each couch. We usually had two to four people staying with us. Now we have up to six people at a time. We quickly learned the importance of rules!

There were more than a few times that the St. Ben's staff asked us to take someone home with us for the night. It usually ended up being a single female who was just passing through the city.

When we take someone home, we offer a home-cooked meal, a bath, a change of clothes (when we have it), we wash their dirty clothes, and provide a safe place to rest. We have absolutely zero tolerance for violence or name calling. We expect everyone to treat and be treated with respect in our home.

Some people stay for a few days, and some stay a few months. We've found that we have to kind of "retrain" some people for inside living. We require people to regularly bathe (which a few have rebelled against). We also require a person to clean up behind themselves (which is also a problem for some). We expect everyone (John and myself included) to get up in the morning. Right away everybody does one chore. The house is cleaned for the day. As I mentioned, we clean up behind ourselves throughout the day. Monday through Friday everyone needs to leave the house to pursue employment, school, or drug and alcohol treatment. Our address and phone number is for people to use on applications or whatever other business. It is also an address for them to receive their mail. Everyone in the house buys food. We all eat together.

I'm not going to lie and say that everyone who came to stay with us has gotten themselves together. I would love to say that everyone is going to live "Happily Ever After," but that isn't the way the streets work. The truth is that most of the people who come through our door will get some rest and then go right back out.

We've had about four couples stay with us. I was hurt when I learned that two out of these four couples had a woman being mentally and physically abused by her mate. You find out who people really are when you live with them.

The majority of women who came to stay with us were prostitutes. I am in no position to judge anybody. All I can do is pray for them to be able to get away from that life the way I did. Almost every woman suffers from some form of mental illness. They also make up the majority of the homeless female population. It breaks my heart. This is the reality of the streets.

We've had some single men stay with us. One of our former single male residents has passed away at a regrettably young age. Whether you liked him or hated him, he will never be forgotten. We love you! God bless you, Bro! One of the other single males is a story all his own! Let's just say that he has a Dr. Jekyll and Mr. Hyde personality when he drinks. He has mental health issues.

We've also had two different elderly men stay with us. One of them is a veteran. They are both repeat residents in our home. I worry most about them when they leave. They also suffer from mental illness.

I don't know if you've noticed the common theme when talking about these people. Most of them are dealing with mental issues. I look around and see how rampant mental illness is in the homeless community. I find it overwhelming when I consider how many people need help out here.

Politicians are always talking about the middle class workers. Some focus on corporations. Nobody ever talks about helping the poor if they get elected. It's usually the aid to the poor that's the first thing cut out for budget reasons. Have you ever wondered why shelters only let a person stay there for thirty to ninety days? Let's be real for a minute. In this economy, it is way harder to find a job. Can you honestly say that you could find a job, save rent and security, pay for transportation, and numerous other needs or bills, in just ninety days? Not to mention that you need furniture and household supplies. The reason you only get ninety days is because someone else gets to come in. The higher the turnover rate the more money is made. Keeping people homeless is actually a very lucrative business!

Did you know that?

I guess I will be quiet now. I would put an end on this story, but it isn't over yet.

We recently realized that while we were waiting on God, we were already doing His work by taking people into our home. What a blessing!

8 LIVING CONDITIONS

As I explained before, we formerly homeless often end up getting bad land lords. That is exactly what I want to tell you about. I've talked about our first apartment already. The next story talks about how, even three and a half years later, John I are still dealing with bad landlords.

I talked about our two bedroom apartment in another story. I mentioned that it wasn't that nice. I'm going to explain that statement. Keep in mind that most homeless people end up in the same living conditions; if not worse.

Many homeless people have evictions or a lack of rental history. It's almost impossible to rent something decent. So, we thought it was our lucky day when we found an apartment. They did no background checks. Cash was good for them. They didn't even charge the full deposit. I wasn't thrilled to be on the third floor with no elevator, but I figured a year here would give us good rental history; or at least a start. We met the building manager. He was nice. The building was clean and quiet.

About two months later, I started getting bit at night. Every time we turned on the light we didn't see anything. It was the middle of the night one night and I was getting bit a lot. I had John go to the light switch. As he turned on the light, I jumped up and snatched the blanket off the bed. And, there crawled eight huge bed bugs! They had been dining on me all night! They were full.

We threw away our mattresses, bought bed bug poison, and mopped the floor with ammonia. I became a bed bug expert. We informed the manager. He said he would tell the owner to exterminate. The subsequent extermination failed to help the bed bug problem.

It took two weeks after the extermination when the biting started again. This time we threw away all of our furniture. So, for a whole year we were at war with the bed bugs. We had to buy furniture four times in that year. It was not only bed bugs. There were cockroaches and mice. There were tons of violations. We didn't even have a working smoke detector.

After all of this, we find out that our nice building manager goes into people's apartments when they are not home. We rigged our door in such a way that we would know if someone had been in our apartment while we were gone. Of course, he had been in our place more than a few times.

We winded up having to call the inspector. When we said our land lord's name, she knew exactly who we were talking about. We weren't the only ones complaining. At least fifteen apartments were having the same problems as we were. Some of them reported that their babies were getting bitten by bedbugs.

We started searching for another place. We had been there for a year. We knew our rental history had improved. We could not figure out what was going on. Prospective land lords kept turning us down. Then, we heard that other tenants were trying to move out. They were upset because the manager was giving out bad reports when a potential land lord would call for a reference. Many people had to make up fake land lords in order to be able to move out.

We also needed to save up to move. We knew that these people weren't going to give us our deposit back. So, we decided to stay our last month on the deposit. They gave us a court date for an eviction for the following month. We knew we would be moving out before any court date. We indeed moved out a week and a half before the court date. We were like many people. We didn't know all of our rights and responsibilities of being a tenant. We didn't know that even though we moved out ahead of time that we still had to show up for court.

A year later we were looking for another place to live and prospective land lords were turning us down again. Finally, one of them let us know that we had a recent eviction on our record. It turns out that we should've shown up for court, after all. They put an eviction on us without us being there.

We just had another bad land lord. Its winter and the pipes froze in our kitchen. When everything started thawing out the pipe busted. The land lord went ahead and cut off the water. She left it that way for over a month. We had to wash our dishes in the bathroom. We had the apartment and in the hallway outside our apartment there were two single rooms and a bathroom like in a rooming house. We were paying for their lights and heat, also. Our bill was over three hundred fifty dollars per month. She has an expensive house and a BMW, but she won't fix anything. So, we decided to move again.

Our eviction is only a year and a half old. We had to find another land lord who doesn't do background checks.

I know that we are not the only formerly homeless people who are going through these problems. You don't even have to be formerly homeless to have these problems, but these problems may potentially make you become homeless.

9 THE STREET CHAPLAIN TOUR

Arn called us one day and asked if we could take him and some of his organization's volunteers in a Street Chaplaincy Program on a tour of the homeless community. They were interested in meeting and ministering to the homeless people. Of course, we said yes right away!

We all met at St. Ben's just as the meal was ending. I was hoping that we could still eat. I wanted everyone to have the experience of eating at a meal site (and it was pouring down rain).

We led the eager chaplains through the door of the church. There were only a few guests left. Most were finishing up their meal. The food on the serving line had already been put away.

Brother Rob (who is with St Ben's) came up and introduced himself. There were leftovers from dinner. The chaplains were able to dine on the infamous chili-mac. They conversed with Brother Rob for awhile. He is a very nice man.

As we came out the door, we were happy to see that it had stopped raining. The sun was coming out on one side, and the thunderclouds were on the other side. I looked up and saw a rainbow. When I looked closer, I could see a second faint rainbow right next to it. The chaplains were just as pleased as John and I to see God's work of art. It was so beautiful that I felt that He was giving His approval for what we were doing. I took a picture, but it didn't compare to the real thing.

The original plan was to go through the courtyard and to a couple of places where people sleep. We entered the courtyard.

The chaplains were in high spirits and ready to extend a loving hand.

The first person we saw was Angie. She was very upset. She told us that she has been drinking and they wouldn't let her eat at the meal site for that reason. I observed her closely. She had a buzz, but she wasn't overly intoxicated. She was upset because she was hungry. She said she only needed one more dollar to get a sub sandwich. She was crying. As she walked away, she said, "I might as well kill myself!" Everyone sprang into action! We took each other by the hand and formed a circle around Angie. We all took turns giving her positive messages. Then, she asked us to pray for her. As we held hands and bowed our heads, feelings of love and peace settled over the group. We took turns praying for Angie. When we were finished, she was feeling better. She was thanking the chaplains when Arn handed her two dollars. She was so touched! She then left to get her sub. I watched her walk away. I wanted to help her so bad! She is one of our many single women.

We walked a few feet and ran into Jesse. He was intoxicated. The first thing he said was, "I need a prayer." We were happy to oblige. Before we were able to start praying, a man and woman came up to us. The chaplains offered to pray with them. They said something smart, turned around, and left. I don't think the chaplains noticed the marijuana blunt in the guy's hand. I was sad as I watched them hurry away. I said a little prayer to myself for them. I remember being like them. I didn't want to hear God's word because I knew I was doing wrong. We turned back to Jesse. We formed our loving circle and prayed. Jesse was grateful.

We never made the whole tour that day. We really only made it a quarter of the way into the courtyard. We were satisfied. We knew that God had sent us Angie and Jesse for a reason. The chaplains had taken their time and listened to their problems. We were able to give them some peace; at least for a little while. Again, I felt sad. I long to do something to help these people who are hurting. For them, there is no silver lining. There is no light at the end of the tunnel.

Only we know the hopelessness of the streets and the fear of being forgotten.

There are no words to adequately describe the feeling.

10 SEARCHING FOR TENT CITY

Arn gave us a call a couple of weeks ago. He and the street chaplains were concerned about the residents of tent city. For those who don't know about "Tent City," I will tell you what I know about it. All throughout the valley, homeless people have set up tents. They are usually in small to medium sized groups. They set up in areas surrounded by trees.

The reason that Arn and the chaplains were concerned is because construction is starting in the valley. Everyone is about to be displaced. The unexpected move would force the homeless to leave most of their belongings behind. And, how are they going to find a place to go at the last minute? The chaplains wanted to warn them and possibly assist them with relocating. We were hoping that the "tent people" would know of another place they could relocate to. It takes a practiced eye to know what spot is good to move to.

Arn had a map of the valley. He knew that some of the people camped out on the near south side, among other places.

We headed to the south side of Milwaukee. I had always known that there were tent cities. I have even lived in one a couple of times. That was years ago. I had no idea where any of the current ones are located.

We got out of our cars and started towards the trees. Our anticipation was great. We were ready to help these people. We walked around in the woods. The ground sloped steeply up and down. Here and there were remnants of previous camp sites.

Walking around those campsites brought back many memories.

41

There were quite a few abandoned campsites.

One site was obviously that of a veteran. There was an almost coffin shaped bed made of branches. The bottom was the ground and the sides were one to two feet tall. If someone were to lay in it, a passerby might walk past and never know that a person was in there.

In my mind's eye I pictured the veteran. I could almost feel his paranoia as he constructed the make shift bed. How long did it take to build it? What was the state of his mind as he built it? Was it somebody that I know? It really made me think. This person had obviously been in war. He is one of our country's heroes. Why is he living in the woods?

We moved on to search out more of the woods. We never did find anybody in the woods. They had all moved on. Staying in the same spot for too long is not a good idea.

I was telling Arn and the chaplains that the tent people were probably at a south side meal site. So, we headed over there. The meal was over for the day. I don't know about the chaplains, but I had already started getting concerned that we weren't going to find them in time. I soon found that concern unwarranted. There were a few people milling about.

Let me tell you how good God is…Out of those few people who were left at the meal site, one person was a tent person. Arn and the chaplains had found him. They told the man about the impending construction. The man assured us that he would warn the others. We were thrilled that we had been able to warn at least one person.

Could you imagine having to leave your stuff behind constantly and unexpectedly? Could you imagine having to relocate all of the time? Being a person on the streets, we lose our cherished belongings all of the time. It never gets any easier.

11 OUR SPAGHETTI DINNER

Every once in a while John and I go to Oconomowoc (and other cities) to speak on behalf of the homeless. We are invited to dinner to eat and get to know the other people. John and I speak about being homeless. Afterwards, there are questions that we gladly answer. Anyway, the last time we went, the dinner was spaghetti, garlic bread, and salad. Everyone ate and talked. The group consisted mostly of teenagers. We always have a good time.

We were getting ready to leave when Colleen (the woman who invited us) asked if we would like to take home the leftovers. We said yes, because we always have plenty of people living in our house.

They came out of the kitchen with three ice cream buckets of spaghetti sauce, an ice cream pail of salad, over ten boxes of spaghetti noodles, a bag of individual salad dressings, and a huge container of garlic bread. John looked at me and said, "What are we going to do with all of that food? I smiled and said, "We'll put the buckets of spaghetti sauce in the deep freezer until Jazz in the Park."

John and I starting bringing food to Jazz in the Park late last summer. Many homeless people are barred or don't feel like walking across town in the heat to get a meal. So, many of our family members are hungry. Jazz in the Park was finally going to start! We pulled one bucket of spaghetti sauce out of the freezer. We added hamburger and John's secret ingredient. We filled a large aluminum pan full of spaghetti. We bought fresh salad mix

43

and tomatoes. I didn't make the salad right away because I wanted it to be fresh. We were just heating the spaghetti up when John's daughter called. She was graduating from high school today. We were supposed to see her graduate and spend a couple of hours with her. After that, we were going to take the spaghetti to Jazz in the Park. We were busy getting everything ready because we had two hours before we had to meet his daughter. Of course, my plans hardly ever work out as I planned!

John's daughter was so excited that she wanted us to come over immediately. We couldn't tell her "no," so we went to her house.

We had been anticipating going to the first Jazz in the Park of the summer.

We watched his daughter walk across the stage. She was beautiful! Then, we went back to her house. We stayed and visited for awhile. When we told her that we were going to leave so we could attend the concert, she told us that she wanted us to stay with her. We couldn't tell her, "no". So, we stayed. By the time we left her house, Jazz in the Park was over. So much for plans!

John and I were talking about when and where to serve the spaghetti. We decided that Saturday would be a good day. On Saturday, supper usually consists of soup and sandwiches. The soup and sandwiches are a huge blessing, but not always filling. We decided that the park on the river would be good because it has picnic tables.

We contacted Arn and Norma and let them know what we were doing. They told us that they wanted to attend the dinner with our homeless family members. We told them the time and location that the dinner would be held.

We loaded up the car with a cooler full of ice and sodas, the pan of spaghetti, plates, watermelon, etc. the plan was that we were going to unload the cooler, food, etc, and leave it with Jenell at the park. John and I were going to go to the courtyard or library to find some people to come have dinner with us. Then, we were going to bring them back to the park with us. That was the plan. Did I mention earlier that my plans never go as planned?

All of a sudden, I had a memory flash of John and me in the courtyard. I was always sick when we were on the streets. John would sit on a bench and let me lay my head in his lap so I could rest. He would watch over me while I slept.

We went into the courtyard and found some people. We didn't have much room in the car, so we invited people to come over to the park on their own. We tried not to invite a large amount of people, because we only had one pan of spaghetti. We let a couple of people ride with us back to the park. We looked everywhere for a parking spot. High school graduation was going on, so all of the parking spots were full. We ended up parking back by the library. I was glad that we had already dropped of the food and cooler. We had to walk from the library. I believe that God had us walk for a reason.

Back in the day, John and I used to hang out in this park every day. I would write while he took a nap. There was a certain way we would always go when we walked to the park. Today was no different.

As we walked in the heat, memories came flooding back. All of a sudden I was homeless again. I remembered every feeling and hardship that we had to endure on the streets. I believe this is what God wanted me to feel.

I hadn't realized it, but I was out of touch with the feelings of being homeless. I have been living inside for almost three years. I honestly feel like I'm spoiled, because I get to go home every day.

We arrived at the park and found about eight people waiting for us. Arn and Norma were already there. Norma had baked some cookies for the occasion.

I sat down right away. I was sitting there talking, but my attention was across the park. I couldn't tell if it was a man or a woman. All I could see was someone sleeping on the picnic table on top of a small hill.

We all gathered together for a picture. After we took the picture, I looked back at the person at the picnic table. He or she hadn't moved.

John said, "Let's pray!" Arn said the blessing over the meal. I silently prayed for the person on the hill.

There were several homeless people in the park, so we invited them to eat. My eyes were drawn to the hill again. I said, "Rob, who is that on the hill?" He said he didn't know. I asked Rob to go invite that person to eat with us.

The person turned out to be a woman. She wasn't as talkative as everyone else. While we were sitting there, my phone rang. It was my aunt. I was telling her how much I loved her, when I glanced over at the woman. She was smiling one of the most beautiful smiles I've ever seen! It looked honest and sincere. Even her eyes were smiling. I had to smile back at her. I couldn't help it! I can't believe that I never asked her what her name was. I just keep seeing her beautiful smile!

Our dinner reminded me of Jesus' parable with His loaves and fishes. We had nowhere near 5,000 people, but way more people were able to eat off of one pan of spaghetti than we ever thought possible. Some people even had second helpings!

Just being able to feed a few hungry people was a humbling experience in itself. I was homeless and hungry once again. God was making me remember everything today. I was definitely out of touch.

When we finished breaking bread, Arn and Norma gave John and me a ride back to our car. I drove back so we could load up the car.

On behalf of the homeless and ourselves, we would like to thank Mr. and Mrs. Valley for making all of this possible.

12 "S"

We met an interesting homeless man quite a few years ago. We were on the streets at the time. For the first few years we didn't talk to him much. And, come to think of it, I'm not sure why. He seemed like a friendly enough person. He was a loner. I wasn't sure for a long time that he was even homeless. He was dressed neatly. He didn't carry a back pack or anything. We would see him around here and there.

I am ashamed to say that I didn't notice when he disappeared. He was gone for a prolonged period of time. Even though I hadn't noticed his disappearance, I definitely remember his reappearance. As soon as I saw him, I realized that I hadn't seen him in a long time.

As usual, I am withholding his name out of respect for him. I only share people's names in the book with their permission. Other homeless people know who I am talking about. In this story I will call him "S".

I decided that there were too many people over the years that I hadn't really talked to. I would see them all of the time, but I rarely said more than "hi" to them as we passed each other. I decided that "S" would be the first person I talked to.

I saw "S" outside the library. I went up to him and said, "It's good to see you back. How are you?" Instead of the usual response, I got a bunch of mumbled words. I hadn't known it, but "S" has a severe mental problem. At first, his words seemed unintelligible, but I found that if I listened closely I could understand him.

"S" appeared pretty agitated. He was smoking a dirty old cigarette butt, so I offered him one of my cigarettes. That one cigarette sealed the deal. We've been friends ever since.

Every time I would see "S," I would give him some cigarettes. He isn't the type to just accept charity. He always has something for me. He gave me a cute spring hat, socks, clothes, etc. If I try to refuse his gift, he gets very agitated. So, I go ahead and accept what he is giving me.

I've had people come up to me and ask, "How do you understand what he's saying?" I tell them, "All you have to do is listen to him."

I started wondering where "S" came from. I know for a fact that he qualifies for Social Security. Why is he living on the streets? I started feeling suspicious. Does he have a payee who is ripping him off? I asked him if he gets a check. He said he didn't know.

I heard through the grapevine that "S" does indeed receive a check. I also heard that "S" got highly upset the last time he saw his payee. He was screaming at her to give him his money. The only problem with the grapevine is that you never know if all of the information is accurate, but it seems to be the case with many mentally ill homeless people and their payees. Does anyone ever check on these payees to make sure that they are doing the right thing?

As for "S", he is still roaming the streets. Although, some other homeless people laugh at him, or pick on him, he always has a ready smile for me. He has his good days and his bad days. Some days he makes more sense than others.

"S" was having a good day when he surprised me. He looked at me and asked me if I was still in school. I was deeply touched. I hadn't thought he noticed nor understood that I am in school.

Good news came at the end of this story. I found out that "S" has received housing, so he is no longer on the streets.

These are the people I want to protect, help, save....

The other day John and I went to the library. We were walking down the sidewalk when John said, "Look who's here!" It was "S"!

Some people like to mess with "S". I think everyone should be kind to the mentally ill, not pick on them. I had mentioned that he had received housing. I'm not sure what program he went through for that. These days he spends most of his days at home. It is a rare treat to see him. I was thrilled to see him! I have a huge soft spot for him.

I sat down at the table with him and he was smiling at me. We gave him a cigarette. He said, "Thanks!" I asked him where he's been. He says, "I've been at home. I've been sleeping a lot." He indeed looked very rested and well bathed. As a matter of fact, his speech was clear. He must be back on his medications again. He looked and sounded fantastic! Thank you, God!

13 NO LONGER WELCOME

I spent many years alienating my biological family. By the time I realized how important family is, it was too late.

Becoming homeless gives me, and others, a chance to become a part of another larger family. We bond over our trials and tribulations. When we need something, we can come to each other for what we need. I could always get help from another homeless person when I was on the street.

I was totally unaware that people's attitudes towards you changes once you get off the street. When I was homeless I was always happy to see someone else find a place to live.

Not everyone feels the same way.

John and I have been off the trail for three years now. And, even though we've kept in touch and didn't forget where we came from, there are those people who no longer consider us family. We are no longer homeless and they still are.

We have opened our door to so many homeless people over the last three years. It hurt my feelings to find out how they really feel. I had known that some people would be envious, but I never thought they would disown us.

I remember spending many cold snowy nights walking the streets. As I passed the houses, I could see the normal people who lived there through the windows. I used to wish it was me who was normal. I never forgot that feeling. I understand why people feel the way they do. I've been there. It's something you never forget. It always hurts to lose a friend.

Many people still care about us. To them, it isn't where we live; it's our bond that counts. We are still able to come to them in our time of need, and they feel free to come to us. These are the friends/family members that we will always cherish. Only we know how it feels to be out here.

14 FAMILIES OF THE HOMELESS

I often refer to homeless people as "lost people." It's almost impossible to locate a specific person on the trail. Some people do hit the streets to get lost. They may have warrants. It's usually over petty crimes. It's rare that a homeless person commits a major crime. When a major crime does happen, it's all everyone talks about. By the time the story gets around, it's a whole new story.

Then, we have those who have been disowned by their families. Many of these people have been dealing with mental illness and drug addictions. Their families get tired of watching their loved ones ruin their lives, so they send them away. I know their family will worry about him or her. Once that person hits the street, they disappear. They are almost invisible.

Some people have told me that they would go home, but they don't want to be a burden. What does that say about your relationship with your family if you feel that you are a burden?

My own mother came from Illinois to Wisconsin several times to identify my dead body. She wouldn't know where I was from several months to a year at a time. I only called her when I was doing well. (This was rarely). I didn't know that she was missing me the way I was missing her. I ended up on life support from contracting MRSA while I was living in a tent. After many wasted years of us arguing or not speaking to each other, she drove from Illinois once again. She was to face her worst fear. She had seen the path that I was on. She continuously begged me to stop doing what I was doing. Mom told me so many times that I was going to die on the streets. The thing that scares me now is that I almost died all by myself. My family was used to not hearing from me for long periods of time. How would they know if I died? I had no identification on me. I would have been called Jane Doe at the hospital and morgue. The only thing that saved me was God almighty. I opened my eyes at one point and said my mother's name and rambled out some numbers attempting to remember her phone number. When I awoke again, my whole family was surrounding the bed. All of the people I haven't spoken to in years. I lived; only to disappear into the streets again to get high.

I know many other homeless people have similar stories. We are lost and forgotten on the streets. We are anonymous. We are nobody. We don't even exist to most people. There's no one to save us; no one to care. What kind of life is this?

15 OUR FRIEND'S SURGERY

Word does travel on the streets. It is a known fact that we take people in and try to help them. People know that they can come to us in their time of need.

This next story gives an example of how we try to help.

We have a friend that we were homeless with for many years. He came to us and told us that he was about to have surgery. He wanted to know if he could come to our house for a day or two until he could get into a shelter. That's where he planned on staying for his recovery. We told him that he was welcome.

The evening of his surgery the nurse called to let us know what time to pick him up. We parked next to the hospital (the hospital is next to the lake). As John and I got out of the car, the frigid lake wind hit us hard. The wind chill was well below zero. I found myself wondering what our friend would have done had he not been coming to our house. He would have had to leave the hospital still groggy from anesthesia and weak from surgery. He was a couple of miles away from his blankets. Could he have even walked that far? Nobody knew about his surgery. No one knew to check on him. What would have happened to him? Would he have lived through the night? If he did make it, how long would it take to get into a shelter? Would he have to recover from surgery on the streets?

I knew another homeless man who had brain surgery and was

released to the streets in the middle of the winter after only a week of recovery.

How many more homeless people can say that they've been through the same thing? Quite a few, I imagine. Could you imagine being weak and tired after surgery? Then, you have to sleep in the snow?

We brought him to our house. Our extra bedroom happened to be empty, so we let him go in there. I really didn't want him to go to the shelter. We felt that he'd be more comfortable at our house.

After a couple days of rest, he came to us and said, "Many people act like they're your friends, but they aren't. You and John are really my friends." He also said, "I'm going to try to be out of your house in a couple of days. I don't want to be a burden." We told him to stay until he healed. We assured him that he was no burden. He told us that nobody had ever cared about him the way we have. That was such a blessing for us to hear that.

That means so much to us. We just want to thank God for allowing us to help people.

16 IS ST. BEN'S HAUNTED?

John and I had an experience when we were homeless many years ago that we'll never forget.

I broke my foot falling down after an ice storm. I had attempted to get into a shelter. Their elevator was broken, so they didn't want to let me stay. They called me a liability. They told me that if they had a fire that I wouldn't make it down the stairs fast enough. I repeatedly tried to tell them that if a fire did indeed occur, I would run on my broken foot or slide down the stairs on my butt. (I was reigning champion of the "butt-sliding-down-the-stairs-game" as a kid). They still refused to let me in. They sent me back out into the snow on my crutches. It was eight o'clock at night and it was snowing. I had counted on being able to stay. Instead we ended up sleeping outside in the snow.

The next day we went to St. Ben's for dinner. I told Brother Dave how the shelter had turned me away. He was kind enough to let us sleep in the meal hall at night until I healed. It was our experiences in the meal hall at night that I feel compelled to write about. Thinking about it still gives me goose bumps.

St. Ben's used to be a boarding school for African American children a long time ago. There's a lot of history there.

The first couple of nights John fell fast asleep right away. I have problems falling and staying asleep. Any little sound will wake me up. I have nightmares and I don't sleep deeply. That comes from childhood and from sleeping outside.

I would lie there next to John and listen to the church. I heard the usual settling noises and knocking pipes. Then, all of a sudden I hear what sounds like someone stomping their foot at the far end of the church. The next stomp is a little closer. By the third or fourth stomp, I realize the sound is getting closer every time. Even though the sound is very loud, John is still fast asleep. I'm trying not to panic. It's still coming closer. My heart is racing. I wonder what's going to happen when the sound of footsteps makes it to us. I hold my breath and pray.

The last stomp was pretty close. If anything is going to happen, now is the time…

It seemed like an eternity before anything happened. There was another stomp and another. Thank our wonderful Lord in heaven that the stomps were now heading in the other direction!

I hadn't been telling John about the sounds in the church. I half thought that it was my imagination.

One night I swore that I heard a woman cough. Again, I doubted myself. John was sound asleep. How could he not be hearing this?

The next morning John and I were folding our blankets when he said to me, "I thought I heard a woman coughing last night. I think this church is haunted." That's all he had to say! I told him about the woman coughing and the stomping.

That night John stayed awake with me. We listened to the noises. The stomping noise started. I was glad that I wasn't the only person hearing these sounds.

We used to hang around this other couple. They asked if they could sleep at the church with us for the night. We told them that the place was haunted. They laughed. We let them come.

At around two in the morning our male friend was sitting up. He was listening to the church. He asked us, "What is all that noise?" We replied, "We told you that church was haunted!" He leaned over his girlfriend and woke her up. "Pack your stuff. We are leaving!" "Why is it so noisy in here?" she asked. "Never mind that, we're leaving!" he exclaimed.

They never asked to spend the night at the church ever again.

We were there for maybe two weeks. We became used to the sounds. I knew they weren't there to hurt us. We were in a church after all. What could happen?

Whether it's haunted, or not, St. Ben's will always hold a special place in my heart. They've helped us so much. I also met John at St. Ben's. St. Ben's is indeed a blessing to our community.

17 SOUP AND SANDWICHES

John and I went to the Saturday meal site for soup and sandwiches. I was a little excited before we got there. I always enjoy seeing everyone.

We were standing outside talking to people when security arrived. He came straight for me and put me in a headlock. When he pulled my hair I knew I had been missed. I nicknamed our security friend "Monkey" many years ago. He has toes like a monkey. (I often tell random volunteers that he can peel bananas with his toes).

When John saw Monkey giving me a hard time he came up to say hi. We haven't seen Monkey in quite a while, so it was good to see him.

When we went inside we were allowed to sit at the first three tables. It wasn't quite time to serve yet. We sat around the table talking and laughing with each other. It's like being back home. We've lived with these people for years. Take the man sitting across from me. He is almost constantly cracking jokes or doing impressions. He is quite good and goes to karaoke night or amateur stand-up comedy night and performs. When I made a comment about the three stooges not being funny he took it very seriously. He gave me a history on the three stooges and their effect on people when they came out. It was quite educational.

The volunteers asked us to be silent as we prayed over our meal. As usual, there are always two or three people who talk through the prayer. I find this terribly rude. You don't have to believe in God, that's your problem. You shouldn't disrespect other people's right to pray. It is also disrespectful to the volunteers who donate their time and energy to make sure we eat. They don't have to do it. They owe us nothing. We ate dinner with our family. John teased and played with the volunteers the way he always has. No matter how long someone stays gone, they are always welcomed back with open arms. The same people are still here; a lot of new faces, too.

We have to face it. No matter how many people we try to save, we can never save everybody. There are going to be those who are always going to live on the streets. It's their chosen way of life. There are always going to be those mentally disabled who wander the streets who self-medicate with drugs and alcohol. There are those who are running from the law. There are the ones who are just passing through. They will stay long enough to make some money, and then they move on. There are women hiding from abusive relationships. There are teenage runaways hiding from their families. There are tons of homeless veterans. Homelessness has its grip on people from any walk of life. You never know when it's going to happen. Nobody is immune.

It felt good to be around familiar faces. It was such a good feeling to be around them again. We just want to thank God for blessing us with these relationships.

18 THE WAY IT FEELS TO ME

Most people groan when they have chores to do. When I clean my apartment, it isn't a chore. It's a labor of love. We are in deep gratitude to God for blessing John and me with a place to lay our heads. We are safe at night. Hundreds of people in the city of Milwaukee can't say that. They sleep in out in the elements every night. They are at the mercy of those who choose to harm them.

How is this fair?

There are many people who get upset when they have to spend all of their money on bills or household goods. They would rather spend it on themselves. When I spend my last dollar on bills or household goods, I don't get upset. It is my absolute pleasure to buy things that we need for the house. I feel great satisfaction when I am able to buy everything we need. I have no problem getting broke buying necessities.

To many people cooking is a chore. They would rather make something easy or buy some fast food. I love to cook. I especially love cooking for large groups. I don't want anyone to go hungry.

When we were on the streets I missed cooking and cleaning my own place. I don't believe you really appreciate these things until you've been homeless. I mean, who gets happy when they pay rent? Me, that's who! The everyday things that we take for granted, or the things we don't want to do, are the things missed most when you are homeless. Just having the sense of normalcy back when you get off the streets means so much. It also takes some getting used to.

The next time you dread cleaning the bathroom or cooking dinner, think of those who don't have a bathroom to use. Think of those who have to eat the same meals over and over regardless if they are liked or not, because that's what the meal sites are serving. Picture having to use the same shower as hundreds of other strangers. Does it sound desirable to you?

Maybe then you will appreciate all that God has given you. I hope so.

19 BROWN BAG LUNCH

Recently, John and I were riding around running errands. His cousin decided to ride around with us. We stopped by the library and happened upon the dinner line that serves bag lunches on the last Saturday of the month.

They line up tables on the sidewalk to serve the food and give away small hygiene items. They have fantastic bag lunches, chicken noodle soup, and hot apple cider.

John and I don't always partake of the free food, but today was a different story. We were happy to see the volunteers due to the fact that we hadn't eaten all day. John and I both got a bag lunch. His cousin opted to buy a sandwich at a restaurant.

She made the comment, "You should have left that food for someone else." I explained that John and I often bring homemade dinners of pork chops, spaghetti, etc. to our homeless family members. John's family in Milwaukee knows that we take people in and are very involved with the homeless people here. His cousin was from out of town. I hope she didn't think badly of us.

I never thought about what we would look like accepting free food when we are no longer homeless. Not everyone knows about the things that John and I try to do for our homeless family members. To them it probably looks bad. John and I are comfortable accepting as well as giving free food. We will absolutely never forget where we came from. We don't always take the free food, but we sure aren't too proud to eat it.

20 ON MY WAY TO THE LIBRARY

I haven't been writing that much the last couple of weeks. I realized that I needed some inspiration. John and I decided to go to the library. That's where many homeless people spend their day.

I got out of the car and made it as far as the sidewalk in front of the library. We ran into "Newport Tone." We saw that he was on crutches. He was having problems with his knees. Lack of insurance is a common occurrence in the homeless population and Tone is no exception. He was able to have the water drained off his knees, but is unable to pay for his pain medication. He is hurting. Once the library closes where is he going to rest? How is he supposed to heal? How long is the pain going to last? It's getting a little warmer outside, but basically, it's still cold outside. How is he supposed to get up and down on the hard ground when he goes to sleep? I told him to speak to different sources where he might get help getting his pain medication. Everyone has already turned him down.

This happens to homeless people all of the time. They are just left to suffer.

I looked around the group of men standing outside of the library to see a familiar face. It has to be over ten years ago that a bunch of us were sleeping on a porch of an abandoned house. There could be twenty of us on that small porch each night. We even had a mattress. There's supposed to be safety in numbers, but sometimes you aren't safe with your own group. One night two guys got drunk and started arguing. They were getting ready to fight when a third man intervened. He was trying to keep the peace. That's when one of the two drunken men cut the third man with a knife. His arm was wounded in the altercation. Thankfully, it wasn't worse. He remembered me and we talked about the past. He showed me the scar on his arm.

I didn't ask, but I believe my friend still sleeps outside.

I enter the library. I get about a quarter of the way into the building and there's another person I recognized. I asked him how he was doing. He started sharing with me that he had been homeless and is now off the streets. As he reminisced about his life, I took out my notebook and started taking notes on what he was saying. He prefers to remain anonymous. He talked about staying at the men's shelter. He felt that it reminded him of prison or the house of corrections with the bars on the windows and the rows of beds. He also talked about curfews that shelters have. He said, "I'm a grown man and I have to be in bed at 9:00 p.m. even on the weekends." He told me that he had been in a Huber jail where they were allowed to stay up all night on the weekends. He shared that he felt freer in jail than in the men's shelter. We were discussing the other men at the shelter and he said this, "Most of them that have been living in the shelter for a long time have no ambition. They're comfortable."

"I worked in food service for most of my life. That's what I am trained to do. I'm a trained cook," he tells me. "I worked for Marquette University for over fifteen years." I was disturbed when he told me how he was treated at a local meal site. "I received a public drinking ticket from the police. The beer only cost me two dollars, why would I pay for a two hundred dollar drinking ticket? I decided to do community service to get rid of the ticket so I wouldn't go to jail. The meal sites are a great place to do community service. As I said before, I am trained in food service. I was serving in the soup line. Homeless people were reaching into the bowls to help themselves instead of waiting for me to hand the food to them. I knew that this was unsanitary, so I was telling them to stop doing it. I was asked to leave by the supervisor. He said that I had a bad attitude. I thanked him and went about my business. I knew I was right. How could I, in good conscience, continue to serve food in unsanitary conditions?"

As always, when talking to a homeless person or formerly

homeless person, I can imagine their life the way it was before they became homeless. I see the hard lessons and hard experience in their eyes as they share their story. They just need one person to listen; one person to care.

Each one of these men gives us something to think about. In our mad rush we call our life we seldom stop and think about things we take for granted. You can get your pain medication after a medical procedure. You have a place to recover after surgery. Do you worry about your safety when you go to sleep? Probably not.

Make sure you appreciate what God has given you and thank Him every day. Try not to be selfish. You don't have to give until it hurts, but you do have to give graciously.

21 THEY DON'T WANT TO LISTEN

We've had over thirty people stay with us over the last three and a half years. When you have a lot of people in one house, rules are needed. John and I offer structure. We expect people to be productive. We try to steer them in the right direction. The problem is that most people don't want to listen. We understand that these people are coming in straight off the streets. It takes a while to shake off that street mentality. We help them readjust to inside living. Regular bathing and chores around the house are mandatory. We give them a little time. Then, after some rest, they are to get up and look for a job. We provide the address and telephone. If they can't work there's school or drug and alcohol classes or rehabilitation. We give them an opportunity to face their issues head on. We are there to guide them.

Usually one of two things happens when we try to help someone. They either cut and run, or they stay for a little while.

Many have good intentions. They start off in a positive mode. They work hard to become successful. They will acquire a job and go to work every day. Or they will head off to school with an arm full of books. Everything seems like its going good. They hang in there for awhile; some longer than others. When we ask them what they've been doing they assure us that all is well. We find out that things aren't the way they seem from the other roommates. We've been lied to by not only this person, but others we've tried to help as well. They lost their job. They are back to using drugs and alcohol again. They are tired of following the rules. Maybe they are stealing from us.

Why do we continue to help people? Time after time we are disappointed to see someone head back out into the streets. The answer is that God told us to do it. He told us to love and care for one another. It took John and I both a thousand second chances before we got it right. If God hadn't intervened on our behalf, we wouldn't be here today. You never know who may be the one to take our help that will better them. We want to be the people who help give someone their life back. We can't, in good conscience, leave people to suffer when it is our duty to love and protect them. It's not right.

22 THE CASINO

I was just thinking about how the circumstances in our lives have drastically changed for us. Things are so different now than when we were homeless. We were on drugs and alcohol really bad before John got shot. We never had money for anything else. The gunshot cleaned John and me up. We no longer use that stuff. So, when I get my check I feel rich. First, we pay our bills on time. I can go to the store and get everything we need for the house. And, if I'm careful, I still have some money left for the month. It's not a lot of money, but it's enough for me.

Sometimes, John and I go to the casino. We may only spend forty dollars apiece. While we are at the casino we see quite a few homeless people. The casino is a good place to stay warm and dry. They are open all night and there are free sodas or coffee. The casino security doesn't mess with the homeless unless they are misbehaving.

Tonight we were at the casino and our friend Bo came up to us. We haven't seen him for a long time, so it was good to see him again. I don't know if he is still homeless or not. I have to say that I was feeling a little guilty because I was gambling and Bo didn't have anything. He was cheering us on. I had to leave my seat to get some change, so he saved my chair for me. When I came back he asked me, "Can Bo get a dollar?" I could smell the alcohol on his breath. I gave him the dollar with no hesitation. I sat back down and started gambling again. In no time I won thirty dollars. Bo saved my chair again. When I got back I gave him five dollars. He didn't ask for it. I just wanted to share. He said, "You guys are really my friends." He hung around for quite a while cheering us on.

We saw several other familiar faces at the casino. While it's a good place to stay warm and dry, you can't lie down and get any sleep. You have to stay awake. The next day there is nowhere to lie down and catch up on your sleep. You have to walk the streets all day exhausted.

I remember those days and thank God almighty that we don't have to do that anymore.

23 TONY

I mentioned before that we had a couple of elderly men stay with us. Both have stayed with us repeated times. Tony (not his real name) has stayed with us quite a few times. He usually stays from one to two months. He gets a check every month, but he doesn't stay in one place very long. He can't seem to put down roots anywhere.

Tony is about 76 years old. He is absent minded. He is forever misplacing his stuff, and constantly has to replace his identification card. Tony wanders around all day and goes dumpster diving. What I mean by that is that he goes through the garbage to find things that are worth money. Tony carries a plastic grocery bag to put interesting items into. These treasures are completely worthless to other people, but to Tony they merit further inspection. There's no time right now so he just puts it in his bag of stuff that he's accumulated so far today.

He always finds a spot to go to. He moves around a lot. He's always looking for the best place. When he gets back to his spot, he'll dump the bag out. He goes over each item carefully. I've seen him keep a million random items that other people wouldn't keep. After he examines everything he will throw away some stuff, but he keeps most of it. He does this well into the night due to the fact that he doesn't sleep much. His hygiene is not so good. I've had to argue with him to take a bath. Then, he goes into the bathroom and gets his hair wet. He pretends to take a bath. I don't know why he hates to take a bath so much. After getting into dumpsters all day, getting in a bath should be a pleasure and is a must! Tony is full of stories and fun facts. He is a wealth of information.

When Tony stays with us I have to hide my towels and washcloths or they will disappear. Every time he uses one I never see it again. Like I just said, he suffers from insomnia. He used to rearrange my kitchen every night.

One day I walked into my kitchen and found the bathroom cleaning towel in the kitchen sink. There were dishes drying in the dish drainer. I went into the bathroom and my kitchen dish towel had been used to clean the bathroom. Good old Tony had tried to do some house cleaning. I was touched. I then told him that he's not allowed to wash dishes any more. He said, "Thank you!" I then rewashed the dishes since he had used the toilet rag to wash them in the first place. To be truthful, that freaked me out just a little bit. But he meant well.

The other day John and I were riding around in the car. It was raining out. We saw Tony at the bus stop. We called out to him. He came over and put his bag in the car. Then, he went back to the stand that gives out free cell phones. We went on our way. A while later he called us from his new cell phone. We decided to let him spend the night because it was raining. When we told him that he could stay for the night, he was so happy.

He got to our place and did the usual. He dumped his bag out to sort through his treasures. We made him some dinner and gave him some blankets. He really needs a bath. He sat up most of the night sorting through his stuff.

I know he wants to move in. We can't have people stay with us where we are at. I wish we could. We can let him come on the rainy nights. We'll let him stay for about a week. He's the one we worry about the most. I feel so helpless when he leaves our house. There's only so much we can do. He hates to pay rent anywhere he goes. The reality is that he will probably die outside by himself. This is the reality for most homeless people.

I have to give an update on this story. Tony called us to say that he found a place to live. The woman who owns the place seems to be very nice. The house looks great. We are just so happy that he is in a place that he really likes. I hope he doesn't do the usual thing and move. He can't even keep up with his mail because of how he moves around. God bless him so much!

An update at the publication of this book: It has been a couple of years that Tony has been off the streets. He indeed moved again. He moved directly into another rooming house. At least he hasn't been homeless for a while.

24 LORI AND TERRY

This is our story:

Terry and I (Lori) have been together for 35 years or so. In 1999, our house burned down and we lost my 3 dogs, 2 cats, and nearly my very own son. We were able to stay at a friend's house until the insurance company gave us money to relocate. Then, again, in 2005 we had some trouble with money. We ended up with Terry at his sister's house and me with a supposed friend. This lowdown snake of a human refused to give me my stuff when Terry and I moved to a hotel to live after he found another job. There we stayed until Terry lost the job he had. It had been a pretty good job, too. I had gone to Louisiana for a long stay and this happened when I was gone. I came back and got everything ready to move. The apartment management company took us to court to evict us, but they decided not to put an eviction on our record. I knew we were going to be homeless, so I packed everything we would need for our homeless state. We were stuck; however, as we lived on the 6th floor and the elevator had not been fixed for two weeks. Then, I called my wonderful cousin who helped with, not only what I kept out, but with the storage of the bulk of the items we had. We then left, though, I admit we went back in a time or two as it was very hot. I got sick from the heat and needed cool water. So, now we are homeless. I had a rolling suitcase and several other bag type stuff, blankets, dishes, can opener, etc. you just about name it, I had it. People were amazed when I would just pull

ON THE TRAIL

things out that someone needed. One time we were given a whole pineapple and I pulled out bowls for everyone. I even had the knife to cut the pineapple with. We had taken our cat Louie with us in his carrier. Peeko went with my cousin. I ended up having to take Louie to the Humane Society and made it clear that if they were not able to place him that I wanted to come get him. Due to no power of my own I missed their phone call by a few days. When I got there they told me they had determined him vicious and killed him. Yes, I said killed him because I had also told them that I was homeless and might not get the message right away.

Ok, now two weeks have passed of us getting up at dawn and leaving the place we slept with a few other people. I tried to make friends with them so we could be safer while on the streets. We ate at the local meal sites. We received food stamps, thank God. We used them to buy food and I also bought candy and resold it so I could have food for my cat and other things that food stamps couldn't buy.

One morning we were going to the breakfast meal site when I tripped and fell. I injured my knee pretty badly. It turned out a year later that I had torn the cartilage on both sides of my knee. I made friends with the man in the street outreach van that went around helping people. I called him for help. He came and saw me. He tried to get me off the street, to no avail. He was able to help me the next night. I was behind the church that we slept by and I was in considerable pain. One of the churchgoers found out that I was hurt. He bought us McDonalds, a pillow for my leg to go on, and a few blankets. That was so nice.

The next day I went to a place for homeless women. Terry had to stay out one more night before he was able to go to the vet's place to stay. It was okay, but you could not stay there all day. Since, I could only sleep there I went to a close by park for the day. I only walked to the place nearby that served lunch. My leg swelled worse and worse.

I finally showed the woman in charge what was going on with my leg. She had me stay in that day and the next day she got me into a medical shelter. Terry got into a nice vet's place that would help him get back on track.

I stayed in the shelter for eleven months until I got my SSI due to my back problems and other debilitating problems. I could not work. In 2005 I had a disc bulge in my lower back. The worsening deterioration of the spine made it impossible to work. Once I got on SSI I got a room.

Terry was being trained in a new field in the program. He came to live with me in the room until I was able to get us an apartment.

Terry lost the job that he was training for. His leg had begun to trouble him. They found a blockage that causes problems walking. Terry was unable to work with his other issues. I had him try for his disability and he got it.

For the first time in our lives we are doing very well together. We have four cats. We still have our health issues. Terry needs to have surgery. I also need surgery on my left knee since I tore that one, too. I already had the other one done.

We were one of the lucky people. Not everyone finds help or their pride won't let them find help. A lot of people had mental issues. Drugs and alcohol are their downfall. Some just needed a job.

This experience showed me a different side of this city. I knew it had been here but I never really understood what it really meant. It was a humbling experience for us both, but I think it was harder on Terry.

People are surprised to find out that I lived on the streets with Terry. Our love is deeper and stronger than most. If you truly love someone you do what it takes, whether it's good or bad you will stay with that person; even sleeping on the cement outside.

[Note: This story was written by Lori. These were all her words.]

I just want to say the Lori and Terry are a breath of fresh air. They are kind and down to earth. They are honest and are not out to use anyone. They are quite generous. We are honored to call them our friends. —Laura

25 HOLIDAYS

John and I go to the library almost every day. We talk to our homeless family and spend time with them. This is where our stories for the book come from. They come from the experiences that we have with our homeless family.

The library is one of only a few places that a homeless person can stay in all day out of the bad weather. It is such a huge blessing to have. When it is closed for the holiday, everything else is closed for the holiday also. Therefore, most of the day is spent out in the elements. Could you imagine Christmas sitting out in the snow trying to stay warm? It doesn't sound like much fun.

I keep speaking on the subject because I want you to understand how serious this is.

Homeless people are dying all the time out here. When everything closes down for the holidays what are they supposed to do? Where are they supposed to go? In the summer it isn't so bad. On the other hand, winter is downright dangerous, as we all know.

This Thanksgiving and Christmas, what are you going to do to help a homeless person? And, it shouldn't be just holidays. What about every day?

Think about it...

26 RIVER RHYTHMS 2013

John and I decided to go to River Rhythms this week. Last week was the first concert of the summer, but it got rained out. Parking for the concert is always a challenge. We drove around a little bit and actually found a great spot to park. We were parking the car when we saw a familiar face. I don't know his name, but he's a really nice man. He's an older man with mental issues.

He and John had the same grizzly bear walking sticks. That's how they bonded with each other. The problem with the grizzly bear stick is that the head falls off. That's what happened to our friend's walking stick. John had gotten a nice hand carved walking stick with a dog head on it from a close friend of the family. John no longer needed a walking stick so he gave it to the man. What made it special was that the stick meant a lot to John. That was about four years ago.

As I was parking the car, I reminded John about the stick. We saw that he was carrying the same walking stick that we had given to him many years ago. We were touched that he still had it. John talked to him for a little while then we went on to River Rhythms.

We went to the "homeless table" and found out that a female friend had gotten kicked out of the park already. I don't know what she did, but I heard that she was really drunk.

I was sitting there looking around for the familiar faces of River Rhythms. These are the people we only see during the summer at the concert. The food tent with John and Mary was absent. I didn't see Olive or her family. Honestly, I was disappointed. It's still early in the summer, so we may see them yet.

I looked around at the people at the homeless table. Just about everybody at the table has lived with us at one point or another. Every last one of them has ripped us off. None of them accepted the help we offered to get themselves together. They are still out here. It's sad to see.

We continue to pray for them every day.

27 MY PHONE

There's an older woman who I see around a lot. We've never spoken until today. She approached me and asked me if she could use my phone. It's very warm out and she's wearing a winter coat, hat, and sunglasses. She tells me that I will be blessed since I let her use my phone. For the next thirty minutes or so she tells me about other people who have been blessed after letting her use their phone. You never know who God is going to have you meet. So, I listened to her stories. I don't know if she's homeless or if she has a home to go to. I see her downtown and at the casino quite a bit.

She tells me that she gave up a $150,000 a year job to take care of her sick mother. She didn't want to leave her mother in a nursing home. She says that after being upper middle class for their whole lives that her mother wouldn't be able to make it in a nursing home. That was many years ago. She tells me that in the 1980's and 1990's she was a woman of importance. She was the only woman in her position for the first five years. She was also the only African American person in that position. She often dined with the president of the United States and even attended a diplomatic ball.

I didn't laugh when she was telling these stories. She may very well have lived that life. I found her to be very spiritual. She praised God so much. I got a good feeling from her. It hurt me to see her sound asleep on the bus stop a few days later.

Like I said before, you never know who God is going to have cross your path. You should treat everyone with love and dignity.

The Lord demands it. When are we going to help these people in need?

28 THE PARK

John and I went to the park the other day. We were looking for some of our homeless friends. When we got there we found eight to ten homeless people barbecuing. The picnic table was laid out with food and condiments.

When I came up I commented on how good the food smelled. Nobody offered us a plate and we didn't ask. John and I have brought homemade dinners to the concerts and have barbecued in the park numerous times. We always invite everyone to eat.

There was some alcohol in the cooler. The man throwing the barbecue was sitting on the cooler to keep people out of it. Only people who contributed money were allowed to drink. John and I don't drink alcohol anymore so he asked for a soda. The man was hesitant to give John a soda. I really couldn't understand what the problem was. We always try to help everyone. When we do something, we include everyone. Not just those who have paid money. I really don't understand how short these people's memories are. Just last summer they were eating our food. This summer we can't get a soda from them just because we live in a house.

Like I said before, people treat us differently because we are no longer homeless. They act like we did something wrong by leaving the streets. We are still the same loving, caring people that we always have been. It kind of hurts my feelings sometimes. To think the only thing we had in common was the streets. Now that we have a place to live, we lost so many friends. Thank God not everyone is like that. We still have our close friends. We have bonds that can't be broken by merely living in a house.

29 THE SIGN

I've seen this time and time again. Almost all of the main meal sites are closed on Saturdays. If there are meal sites open on Saturday, then I stand corrected. We only know about the ones serving when we were homeless. I know that they are not in the immediate area. On Saturday there is no breakfast, but there is lunch at 11:30 a.m.

On the first three Saturdays of the month the evening meal is located inside a nearby church. They serve soup and sandwiches. The fourth and occasional fifth Saturday of the month the evening meal is held on the sidewalk near the library. They give you your choice of tuna, egg salad, or bologna and cheese sandwiches. They have great lunches, chicken noodle soup, hot apple cider, and small hygiene products.

Sometimes, only one meal site serves for the whole day. Many people count on the bag lunches and chicken noodle soup. Occasionally, on the fifth Saturday, the church is unable to serve. There will be a sign posted on the bus stop that they are unable to serve that day. I believe that if the church had it in their budget they would have served. They are such wonderful people.

John and I went to the library and got on the computer. I looked at the time. It was 3:15 p.m. In forty-five minutes they would be serving bag lunches and soup next to the library. I was happy because I was starving. At 4:00 p.m. we rushed outside to get in line. On the way there one of our family members told us about the sign posted on the bus stop. I thought he was just kidding. I walked around the corner. There was no line of people, no food. I was pretty disappointed. I had really been looking forward to their bag lunches, but my disappointment was nothing compared to the homeless people's disappointment. I looked in their eyes and remembered when it was I who was going hungry. Now, I could go home and get something to eat. All of these people were going to go hungry tonight.

Our homeless friend made the comment: "Everybody is going to have dinner at John and Laura's house tonight!" If he only knew how much we wanted to do just that. We can't afford to feed a lot of people.

Do you count on a meal site for your meals? What if they aren't open? What if you don't have enough money to buy something to eat? What do you do? Is this something you worry about on a daily basis?

30 LEAVE THE PARK

We were looking forward to River Rhythms this week. We had some errands to run and then we were headed straight for the concert. Summer concerts and festivals are popular places for homeless people to attend.

We were on our way to the concert when we ran into one of our homeless family members. In the last book I mentioned the "homeless photo album" that the police have. It's full of homeless and formerly homeless people.

It was reported to us that a couple of homeless people were causing a problem at the concert. What the police did next was completely unfair to the rest of the homeless people who were trying to enjoy the concert. Anyone and everyone in that photo album were kicked out of the park. The police told everyone, "You are all guilty by association."

How is it fair that everyone is punished for the actions of a few? Holding everyone responsible isn't right. I feel like the homeless were discriminated against because they were homeless. You can't just stick us all together in one group and say that we are all guilty.

John and I had been looking forward to spending time with everyone. We felt that the concert wouldn't be the same without our homeless family, so we didn't bother to attend the concert this week.

31 GAMBLING

During our times at the casino we saw many homeless people there. As I mentioned before, the casino is a great place to stay warm and dry during bad weather. You can't beat having free soda and coffee either! We can completely understand their motive for being there.

The whole situation saddens us, but we saw something that was further troubling to us. There are some homeless who get Social Security, or other income, and they are gambling. They aren't gambling just a little bit. They are spending their whole check. At first I thought, "Why are they gambling if they are homeless? Shouldn't they use their money to get a house?" Then it occurred to me: maybe they are homeless because of their gambling.

I've seen it take over people like it's an addictive drug. They can't stop until it's gone. We've even seen one of our friends win $900 and he also had about $500 left from his check. A few days later he needed to borrow some money from us. I couldn't believe that that much money was gone that fast.

There's another woman who camps out that we see there, also. She's been homeless for quite a while. We've known her for many years. I didn't know she had an income until I saw her gambling.

We talk about drug and alcohol addiction all the time. We don't address gambling enough. It's just as addictive as drugs.

It was only a few homeless people who we saw gambling, but we still worry about them.

It's not for us to look badly upon them. It's for us to help them.

God would want it that way…

32 THIRTY DAYS

I am giving you one example on how a person becomes homeless.

We have a friend who was living in a house. He had a roommate. There were also other people living there.

He had renting there for quite some time when the landlord unexpectedly sold the house. He totally disappeared. Everyone in the house was given thirty days to get out. How do people on a fixed income gather together rent and a security deposit in just thirty days?

Do you understand that there are many different reasons that people are homeless? It's not always their fault.

We read another story where a couple lost their house due to a fire.

You just can't stereotype everyone.

Think about it…

33 KEVIN AND LORI

John and I were in the casino one night. I went to get us a soda. I saw a familiar bandanna head moving away from me in the crowd. He has worn the same one on his head for years. This was someone we hadn't seen in a long time. I had a hard time catching up with him. He is pretty fast! I finally caught up with him and tapped him on his shoulder. When he recognized me, he put me in a sort of head lock and planted a wet kiss on my cheek. It was one of our homeless friends named Kevin.

We go way back with Kevin. I don't even know how to put this story into words. There are too many memories to even recount here.

We met Lori first. She was really quite witty. I could sit with her for long periods of time if she was in a good mood. I tried not to bother her when she was agitated. Lori was very generous, but if she got down to her last she would tell you to go get your own! She was very "no-nonsense." I grew to really care about her. She was quite the drinker. She always put her alcohol in a soda can or juice bottle to hide it. The police knew about her little trick, but they usually didn't bother her about it. She rarely caused any real problem. It was when someone had been egging her on or antagonizing her that she would snap.

She often slept by John and I for safety reasons. She would be alright for a couple of days. Then, she would venture off by herself for a few days. We always worried about her being alone, but we couldn't force her to stay with us.

She would always tell us that she was waiting on her Kevin to get out of jail. John and I hadn't met him yet. Everything we knew about him was because Lori told us.

When Kevin got out of jail, we could tell right away that they were made for each other. They were both short. They were so cute together! Kevin and Lori would drink together and they would sometimes argue, as most couples do, but one thing was for sure: Kevin would never hurt Lori in a million years. As a matter of fact, Lori would listen to nobody but Kevin when she was agitated. He was the only one who could touch her. She was sick. Kevin would take care of her the best he could.

One day they had an argument. Kevin left for a couple of days to cool off. During that time Lori passed away in a park from a massive stroke (I'm not sure if park is accurate. I also heard that she passed away in detox. You never know with rumors). When Kevin learned of her death, he was devastated. It's been a few years, but his eyes still fill with tears when he speaks of her.

Seeing Kevin at the casino brought back so many memories of being on the street. Kevin only had one dollar to his name. He told me, "This is the only dollar I have. I want you to gamble it. If you win, that's good. If you lose, that's okay, too." We didn't win anything. That was okay. I was touched that he would offer his only dollar to try to win us some money.

We talked about Lori. I told him, "You know, she really loved you." He said, "I know. I loved her very much, too." He sniffled and wiped his eyes. I told him that we had a picture of Lori in the first book. He said he really wanted to have a copy. We knew that he couldn't afford to buy a book, so we were going to give him one for free. He told me that he needs a picture of her because she is fading in his memory. We agreed to meet in two days for him to get a copy of the book.

He hung around at a nearby slot machine. I could see him dozing off. I knew how tired he was. I wanted so badly to take him home with us, but we aren't in a position to take people in right now. Our living conditions aren't the best.

As we left, I said a little prayer for him. I felt so helpless. I hate feeling like that.

He never showed up to get the book. We don't know where his camp is. We don't know where he hangs out. We don't know who his friends are. He is anonymous. We have to wait until we bump into him again.

    Until we see you again, Kevin, God bless you!

34 SHE IS STILL HOMELESS

It just breaks my heart. There are these long time homeless people who can't seem to get themselves together no matter what they do. Our friend in the next story struggles constantly with mental issues and alcoholism. That would be the self medicating that I talk about a lot regarding the mentally ill. I've seen her go through long periods of sobriety only to fall back into drinking. She gets a social security check every month. She often lives at the motel. I'm not sure why she doesn't have a house. All I can tell you is what she told us.

Many years ago she started dating one of our close male friends. They've been together for almost as long as John and I. They go through many problems, but they stick together for the most part. We were on the streets with them for quite a few years.

The other night, John and I stopped by the park where we know quite a few homeless people are sleeping. There were a lot of men and only a couple of women in the group. One of the females is our friend that I was telling you about. When she came to the car she was quite tipsy. We hadn't seen her for a long time. When we last saw her she was sober. I was disappointed to see her drinking again. I don't want you to get the wrong idea about her. She is a sweet, generous woman who gets taken advantage of all the time. She is a good friend to have because she is a nice person.

My other concern was that she was one of only a couple of women in a group of men. Homeless men are not rapists by nature, but there are aggressive men in every population. There are some men who would take advantage of drunken women on the streets.

The women are too afraid to report it anyway. So, I was glad when she asked for a ride to where her son is staying. (This happens to be a motel). It's quite far from downtown. You have to take the bus or car. It's way too far to walk.

She got in the back seat. As soon as we pulled off she was telling us that she needs a payee. She wanted one of us to do it. We are not able to be anyone's payee, so we had to tell her no. We helped give her some ideas on where she could get help. According to her, she is owed back money for the time she hasn't had a payee. She went on to say that she and her man broke up because he is using drugs. We haven't seen him in a long time and he wasn't there to defend himself, so we took it all in with a grain of salt. If he is using, John and I can relate. We went through many years using drugs, so we can understand another who is struggling with it.

She is homeless again. When we took her to her son, she had to sneak in the back door. My heart goes out to her. What if she ended up spending the night in the park? Would she have been raped?

These people need guidance. They need the resources to get complete care. They need help to become completely independent and self-sufficient. We need to address all of their issues.

This is the type of facility we would love to open. Would you consider donating time or money to open such a facility?

Please, think about it! God bless you!

35 THE STRAP

When we showed up downtown today, our friend came up to our car all agitated. He told us that a drunken stranger was harassing him.

Our friend is a loner. He stays to himself. He doesn't bother anybody. He actually goes out of his way to avoid trouble. That is what he did in this situation. When the man started harassing him, our friend walked away.

Our friend is not a fighter. He is small in stature. He is going on sixty years old. His fighting days are behind him.

He told us, "I walked away from that man and he followed me. He pushed me. He put his fists up to fight me. So, I snatched my belt off and started hitting him with it!" Our friend said that the attacker was surprised when he got hit with the belt.

I'm not mad at our friend for defending himself. He didn't even know the man. We don't even know if the attacker was homeless or not.

Could you imagine how scary it is to be alone on the streets? You never know where danger will come from next.

36 THE QUEST CARD

I had meant to write about this a while ago. I heard that there was a man coming to the meal sites. He had a Quest card machine in his vehicle. If you don't know what a Quest card is, I'll tell you. It is a card that resembles a credit or debit card and it has food stamps on it instead of cash. What he would do was swipe a homeless persons Quest card on his machine. If there was $200 in food stamps on the card, the man would give the homeless person $100 in cash. In other words, the homeless person would always get half for whatever was on the card, and the man would keep the food stamps.

At first, I was upset with the homeless people for giving up their card. Even though there are meal sites, food stamps are still needed for the times that no one is serving, or when the food at the meal site can't be eaten due to being on a special diet, but I also remember how desperate we were for money when we were on the streets. We did basically the same thing. So, we can't get mad.

Then, I thought of the man with the machine. He came to the meal sites with the intention of victimizing the homeless people. He knew what he was doing. He knew that they were desperate for money.

The good news is that I heard that he finally got caught. We haven't really thought about him since.

Then, just recently, I overheard a conversation that all of the homeless people who participated in the food stamp incident are being barred from getting food stamps for a whole year.

As a former homeless person, I don't know how to feel about it. On one hand, they need to face the consequences. On the other hand, I worry about them going hungry. Yes, it's their own fault. I just keep remembering my own feeling of desperation when I was on the streets. Desperation drives you to do things you wouldn't normally do.

37 ON THE CORNER

A couple of days ago John and I were leaving the library. Homeless people kept stopping us to talk as we left. Quite often we end up giving someone a ride somewhere. John and I try to help people when we can. They can be homeless people, family, or even strangers. We don't have much, but we do what we can.

I try to be honest as I can in these stories. I have to give praise to the Marquette University security police and I'm going to tell you why.

As I said, we were leaving the library. We were half leaving, half talking to everybody. From across the street I hear a male yelling, "John, John!" He came running across the street. He is a young homeless man that we know. He's most likely not more than 21 years old. Tears were streaming down his face. "Can you take me home, Laura? John, please take me home!" He was distraught. He and his girlfriend had been arguing. He was trying to get away from her. He did the right thing by leaving the situation. I believe it is important to mention at this point that they are an interracial couple like John and me. He is African-American and she is white. I mention this because it helps you understand why the young man feels the way he does in this situation.

As the young man came across the street to ask us for a ride, the Marquette University security showed up. Immediately, the young man went on the defensive. He expected them to blame him for everything and you could tell by the way he acted. He kept telling them over and over that he had done nothing wrong. He was sobbing. He kept begging us to take him home. I think he meant his parents house. He and his girl have been on the streets as far as I know. John and I tried to calm him down, but he was hysterical. He just knew that he was going to jail.

Through all of this, the security officers remained calm. They didn't attempt to subdue him. They let him walk freely about. They made no sudden moves.

I have to admit that part of the reason I stayed was because I wanted to see how the officers handled the situation. I hear homeless people complain about aggressive officers. I wanted to make sure it was professionally handled.

The young man was begging to be let go. Security kept trying to explain that they had to wait for the police department to show up. Still, they were completely calm. I was impressed. It took awhile for the police to show up. Security maintained their professionalism throughout the whole ordeal. The young man calmed down a little.

When the police department showed up, the young man started getting agitated again. He really was afraid that he was going to jail. Security went over and discussed the details of the case with the police. They were of the opinion that the young man did nothing wrong. The police came over and told him that he should stay away from his girlfriend for the night. This way they could calm down. They told him that he was free to go.

I believe everything was professionally handled. Thank you Marquette University security and Milwaukee police department!

38 THE LINE

We were waiting in the soup and sandwich line. The church was running a little late. Homeless men and women volunteered to unload the food and tables from the bus like they do every time. I was excited about the tuna sandwiches. I was in a great mood! The sun was shining. Everyone was talking and laughing; everyone except one person. I don't know who he was. I do know that I was going to tell him about himself!

This is how it almost went down: the church people were moving kind of slow and they were a couple of minutes late. As far as I was concerned, they could take as long as they wanted. There was plenty of food and everyone was going to get some. Besides, it was free and very good! These people obviously put a lot of love into their food. They didn't have take time and energy to feed us in the first place.

From directly behind me I hear, "What the ### is taking so long?" I was a little irked, but I didn't say anything. John and I continued our conversation. A few minutes later the man said very loudly, "What the ### is the holdup?" I don't know if the church people heard him. I started getting very agitated. I don't know if he was drunk or what. I felt that these lovely people didn't deserve to be talked to like that.

The third time the man cursed out loud I spun around to face him. I opened my mouth. John knows how I am. He immediately stopped me. I was about to tell that man about himself!

Just then, the line started moving. It's a good thing for that man that there were two tuna sandwiches with my name on them!

On the serious side, never take a volunteer's time or energy for granted. We are all adults, these people are not obligated to feed us. They do so out of love and compassion.

Please, always respect our volunteers. They are angels from God.

39 IN THE 90S

We watched the weather report on the news this morning. The weather man said there was going to be a heat index well into the 90s. John and I are on medications so we can't be in the heat. We don't have air conditioning in our apartment, so we were trying to decide what to do. We go to the library a lot, but we wanted to do something different. We decided to go see where the homeless people stayed cool besides the library.

When we got to the park there were a couple of nice size groups of homeless people there. One group was in one area of the park in the pavilion and the other group was in another area in the shade. We knew the people at both tables. I chose the table where my best friend of many years was sitting. I hadn't seen her in a long time, so it was good to see her. She is not homeless anymore, but she comes out to visit for a couple of days at a time, here and there. There were a lot of different personalities at the table, but somehow it all worked. You could sense the closeness of the group.

The homeless hustle every day. Some days are fruitful; some are not. When everybody comes together, whoever made the money today buys the beer and sometimes a bag of weed. At this point I should remind you that I am honest in these stories. Although, I am honest, I do not get anyone in trouble. I also don't want you to look badly upon these people. They need to escape reality when it is too hard to face. They know no other way to cope.

The feeling around the table was one of family. Everyone was talking and laughing. It felt really good to be there. It was like old times. Just like the old days, I sat there and worked on the book. I then remembered that there used to be biting flies in this park. They bite your legs while you sit at the picnic tables. I asked my friend if the flies were still there and she said, "Yes, that's why we are sitting on the table instead of at the table!" A few minutes later they started biting like crazy! Homeless people were feeding the seagulls and the geese some bread. Everyone was drinking and a few were smoking weed. Everyone was getting along and they were cleaning up behind themselves.

This may not seem like the right thing to be doing when you are homeless, but what else is there to look forward to? Could you imagine your life becoming so hopeless that you only have beer and weed to look forward to?

Our little gathering broke up in the usual fashion; the police showed up. The officers walked up and said, "No drinking, no weed smoking. Get your stuff and move around!"

They didn't ask for any identification from anyone or run any names. They already knew who everyone was. They did a sweep of the park kicking out all of the homeless people. When you kick homeless people out of one park, where do you suppose they go? To another park! They don't have a lot of choices.

40 THE NEXT DAY

We had such a good time at the park; we decided to go back the next day. All of the same people were there plus a few others. A few of them were playing dominoes. Today I wore pants to keep from getting bit by the flies. I brought my notebook with me, as usual. Everyone is used to me writing. I've been doing it for years. All I have to do is listen to everybody talk and watch them interact with each other. There is always a story to tell.

The particular group that we are with doesn't drink before the afternoon. Everyone is up and dressed super early in the morning. Sleeping in is not an option on the streets. Each person in this group takes care of the others. When one person has something, they all have something.

I have an example. When you are drinking beer outside you have to know what public bathroom you can use. After using it for so long, they usually end up stopping you from using it; which is what happened to the next lady who I'm writing about. My friend "J" had been using the same bathroom over and over. After so long, they stopped her from using it. I think that as long as we aren't making a mess or camping out in the bathroom, we should be able to use it. Anyway, they told "J" that she couldn't use their bathroom anymore, so she had to find another one to use. I don't know about you, but I can't hold it while I walk all over town looking for a bathroom. On her way to find another restroom she found a pack of cigarettes. Eventually, she found a bathroom. When she came back she told her boyfriend about the cigarettes that she had found. There were about ten people sitting at the picnic table. Her boyfriend said to the group, "When I have something, we all have something." He then passed a cigarette to each person. Everyone lit up. I observed the expressions on everyone's faces. For the moment they didn't have to struggle to have something.

This story isn't really about the cigarettes. The story now goes from the way the homeless share everything with each other to the feeling of camaraderie and closeness they share. Their loyalty to each other is fierce and unbreakable. There's nothing like it.

41 WE'RE HUNGRY

There is a homeless couple who frequents the casino. We see them when we go there. They seem nice. Tonight they asked us for some money so they could eat. John and I looked at each other. John said to them, "Come with us." We never let anyone go hungry. We always take homeless people home with us, so taking them home with us was nothing new. We told them they could spend the night.

We weren't expecting company, so I didn't have anything thawed out for dinner. We stopped at an area gas station to get hot pockets, sodas, chips, and snacks. We then headed for home. I gave her a wash cloth, towel, and pajamas to use. We gave them some blankets and a foam mat to make a pallet on the floor. They seemed to be happy that they had somewhere to spend the night. We attempted to watch a movie, but we all kept talking. We found out that neither one of them has a criminal past nor do they have any warrants. We talked to them about attending college. Neither one has attended college. We told them that student loans could provide them with rent and deposit on a place to live. Either one of them could get a decent job with them having no criminal record.

This is where I had to pause. Why are they homeless? There's nothing holding them back besides being homeless. If you are really determined you can get off the streets, barring health problems or having a criminal past. Which is why I'm confused as to why they are homeless. Maybe there's something I don't know about their situation. Maybe all they really need is some encouragement.

The next morning we let them sleep in. We knew that they were exhausted. When we all got up she helped me cook eggs, bacon, hash browns, and toast. We watched the news. The weather man reported rain for the next three days. We told them they could stay on the rainy nights. We had learned that their jackets and bags of clothes got soaked in the last rain storm and were currently hanging in a tree to dry. I told them they could bring their wet stuff to our house and hang it up to dry for the night.

At this point, John and I were seriously considering taking these people into our little apartment. We really wanted to help them. They have so much potential.

John had therapy to attend, so we all left the house. I thought they were going to wait for us at the library. Instead, they wanted to go hustle at the casino. We were disappointed. We waited for their call that night, but it never came. We didn't hear from them for a couple of days. Then, they called and asked if they could spend the night. We told them, "Yes." They met up with us and we all went back to our place.

Again, John and I were talking to them about attending college. They told us that that's what they really want to do. We took that as an indication that they wanted to get themselves together. John and I had been discussing it with each other. We felt that this couple really offers a lot of potential. We told them that they could stay, but they have to attend school and in the near future at least a part time job. We were going to make sure that they got to school or work on time. We had already been feeding them. Then, we found out that she sold her food stamps in those few days that they had been gone. I didn't know how to feel about that. We just kept doing what God wanted us to do.

I went over the rules. We aren't supposed to have anyone staying with us, so everyone has to be really quiet. Clean up behind yourself. Everyone contributes when they can. We all have to go to church. We all have to work together. These are not hard rules to live by. They agreed to the rules. When we left in the morning, they asked to be dropped off by the welfare building. Many homeless people get their mail there. People can also apply for food stamps there. That was a few days ago that we dropped them off. We haven't seen them since. We were so disappointed. We had a lot of hope for them. God bless them wherever they are.

An update at the publication of this book: There was a schizophrenic woman who took us in when we were on the streets. She used to be homeless. She is infamous for taking up to thirty homeless people home with her at a time. She has often gotten evicted and/or was ripped off while trying to save everyone. In this case it was no different. She had taken home the same couple that John and I recently helped. She takes psychiatric medications that put her into a deep sleep. When she woke up, she found her electronics missing. This is the millionth time that she's been ripped off. She will continue to take homeless people home with her. She is kind hearted like that.

42 GOING TO CHURCH AT ST. BEN'S

I mentioned in another story that John and I are barred from St. Ben's and another church. We are "crime bosses" according to rumor. I feel two different ways about that statement. First, I laugh because the idea is ludicrous! We have no money! On the other hand, we are hurt. We are hurt because people who have known us for years actually believed these lies. They should have known better. So we can't go to these meal sites anymore. It has also been my dream to marry John there. That's where we met.

We love to attend church there even though we aren't Catholic. Almost everyone in the congregation volunteers at St Ben's regularly and have been doing so for years. Each person has touched our lives in a special way when we were homeless and to this day. I don't know if they've heard the rumors or not. They sure don't act like they have, because they are always happy to see us.

There's one special volunteer named Sister Margaret. We met her way before John got shot. After he started living at the nursing home to recover, Sister Margaret came to visit John every week. She would tell him a joke every time she came. He always loved her visits. As a matter of fact, many of the volunteers came to see John in the hospital. We were so touched. Everyone shared their love and support through our difficult times. Dozens of homeless people came to see him, also.

We just want to tell Brother Dave and the others that we love and miss them.

Going to St. Ben's means so much. Thank you, God!

43 WHAT HAPPENED TO CAMPUS FOODS?

When we were homeless we would walk all the way to Campus Foods for beer, soda, snacks, etc. Not only were they cheaper than the downtown stores, the staff was also way friendlier. They were nice to all of the homeless people who shopped there. I remember they used to keep John's favorite chips behind the counter until we came to get something. They always talked to us and made jokes. They asked us questions about being homeless, which we answered. Everyone there was excited about the book I was writing (the first one). They were always supportive. They even passed out fliers about the book to customers for us after it was published. It may not seem important to you. The way they treated us was different than the way most people treated us. Campus Foods was an important part of our homeless lives.

I heard that people with shotguns came in and robbed the store. Things were never the same for anyone there ever again. They shortened their hours to day time only. Eventually, they sold the store to the college so they could build an apartment building for the students. When I drive by now all I see is land where the store used to be.

We know that change is inevitable, but we are always going to miss the staff at Campus Foods.

God bless you all!

44 IT'S FALL

Summer is finally over. The days are getting shorter. The oppressive heat of summer is gone. The leaves on the trees are changing color and falling off the trees. Fall is truly a beautiful season. That is, it is a truly beautiful season for those who have a house. For the homeless it is a different story. This is the time of year when we start trying to collect enough blankets to keep warm during the winter. Fall means cold air and colder rainy days and nights. We have wet blankets and wet clothes.

Homeless steal from the homeless quite often. If you have some dry blankets in a garbage bag they are likely to come up missing. You have to check on your stuff throughout the day. The police will also throw away your blankets, clothes, etc. You can't just show up at your spot at night and expect your stuff to be there. You definitely have to know ahead of time that your blankets are gone. That way you can get a few blankets for tonight. It could mean life or death in the winter, and has. We have lost many beloved friends in the winter.

You should pray for the homeless year round, especially in the late fall and winter. They are the hardest seasons to be homeless in.

Thank you.

45 ANOTHER JOHN

Several years ago Baby and I met a man named John. When we would ask him how he was doing, he would say, "No good. My eyes are full of pressure. They are about to pop out." John was sincerely afraid that he was going to lose his eyes. We often saw him eating out of garbage cans. We tried to get John to eat at a meal site. Although he was in St. Ben's parking lot, he refused to go inside to eat. Baby and I brought him blankets and bag lunches. We fed him for a few days before he disappeared.

We were concerned when we didn't see him anymore.

We hadn't seen John in over six years. We recently moved to the south side of Milwaukee. Baby and I were sitting at the bus stop waiting for the bus when a man approached us. He had a thick layer of dirt all over him. Even his face and hair were covered in a dark layer of dirt. He started talking to us. I found him to be very intelligent. He didn't even ask us for anything.

Even though he was dirty and his hair had grown out, I had recognized him immediately. As I was telling Baby that we had met John several years before, all of a sudden John said, "Hey, you guys used to give me sandwiches and blankets!" Knowing his mental state, I was incredibly touched that he remembered us!

I saw that he had a cup of coffee from McDonalds. I didn't know if he was still eating out of garbage cans. I asked Baby to give John five dollars. We wanted to make sure it was enough for a meal. John was thankful and left immediately to get something to eat.

I told Baby that John was the man who used to think that his eyes were going to pop out. Baby was surprised. He hadn't recognized John until I explained it to him. The dirt was a good disguise.

I found myself wondering about John's whereabouts these last few years. I know he qualifies for Social Security. Was he already getting a check? Has his payee been giving him his money or are they keeping it? Why doesn't he have a safe place to live?

There are just so many questions...

I was going to end the story there, but I have an update about our friend John.

We were at the casino the other day. We saw a few homeless people there. They've got some sort of hustle at the casino. I'm not sure what it is.

I spent my twenty dollars and went to see how Baby was doing. I was watching him play when I looked up to see a familiar face. It was John! We hadn't seen him since that day at McDonalds a year ago.

Now we were seeing him at the casino being escorted out by several security guards. When I said, "Hi, John. How are you doing?" he asked me, "Where do I know you from?" In his next breath he exclaimed, "You are the ones who gave me the blankets a long time ago!"

I asked him how he was doing. He told me that security was putting him out because he wasn't gambling. He asked me for a cigarette. I told him that I don't smoke any more. I wish I had thought to give him my change. They led him out.

All we did was give him some food and blankets many years ago when we, too, were homeless. He never forgot. You never know who you are going to touch with your actions. You never know who is going to remember. I wonder how long it will be before we see him again?

May God keep him warm, safe, and fed until we meet again.

46 MY FRIEND

We came downtown yesterday. I saw one of my female friends. I don't see her much, so I was glad to see her. She used to be homeless, but she has a house now. My friend comes out and spends a few days on the trail with her boyfriend, and then she goes home for awhile to be with her kids. There are complex reasons why her boyfriend can't live with her. I won't share that with you, because it's my friend's business. Yesterday she found out that her long time boyfriend had moved on to another woman on the trail. She was obviously heartbroken. I felt for her. She suffers from mental problems, so I worry about her. She has a hard time staying regular on her psych meds. I could tell that she had been on the trail for a couple of days. Her hair was greasy and dirt was caked under her fingernails. She was on the verge of tears. She even admitted to relapsing the night before.

At this point I want to hug her and make all of her problems go away, but I know it isn't realistic. I know that she has to figure it out for herself the way John and I did. I do love her so much.

She had no way to get home after she and her boyfriend broke up. She decided to spend the day and night with us. She was only with us for a few hours before her plans changed. We were in front of the library and there were quite a few homeless people milling about. Someone came up with a hustle. When another of my friends was talking about the hustle quietly to my friend, I was trying to listen. Another homeless person covered my ears to prevent me from hearing what they were saying. He told me that I wasn't homeless anymore, so I couldn't get in on any hustle. I didn't want to anyway. I just wanted to hear what they were up to. I'm not going to tell you what it was. People on the streets are desperate for money and will find many ways to get it.

Anyway, as soon as my friend heard what was going on, she was in. As soon as a way to make money came up, she forgot all about me. I haven't seen or heard from her since.

I just pray that she stays safe and gets herself together.

47 THIEVES

There is a woman who has helped John and me a couple of times during our homeless days. She used to be homeless herself, so she takes homeless people home with her. I mean she has literally invited up to thirty people at a time to sleep at her tiny one bedroom apartment. It's been such a problem before that she lost her place. She is kind-hearted and wants to help everyone. She suffers from a severe mental disorder, so she really bonds with homeless outcasts. What I mean by that is she really identifies with people who are also mentally disturbed. Her case worker helped her get relocated with the condition that no one spends the night at her place ever.

My friend, of course, still takes people home with her, risking her home in the process. She does it more sparingly than she used to. The problem is that she wants to believe that every person she helps is honest and trustworthy. More often than not someone will steal from her; which is what just happened to her, again. She is hurt and angry. She really reaches out to anyone and everyone and they do this to her. The same people have done the same thing to John and me. There's a reason why some people are homeless. They have that predatory mentality when it comes to life. They use everyone. They never have enough. They are downright miserable with their existence. It's really a shame. Most of these people are destined to die on the streets. And, who would know? John and I love each and every one of these people. We just know that we have to be more selective of who we try to help and deciding how much help to give them.

Our friend is going to be blessed in heaven when she gets there for all of the people she has tried to help. I pray that never changes.

48 WHY DO THEY DO IT?

I mentioned in the first book that when some homeless people get their checks they get a room for about a week. The rest of the month is spent sleeping outside.

I remember years ago when John and I used to do the same thing. At that time John was the only one of us with an income. That was back when John and I were heavily involved in drugs and alcohol. When his check would come we would go to the diner, first thing in the morning. After we ate, we would go to the mall and pay our cell phone bill. Then, we were off to get a motel room. We would go to various places on the way, such as the liquor store and the dope house. We usually walked everywhere. Sometimes, we would take the bus. The motel room served as a safe place to get high and drunk for a couple of days. It then served as a place of much needed rest from the streets for the remainder of the week.

This may sound shocking to you. I've always tried to be as honest as possible in my stories. There is a reason why some people are homeless. They most likely will remain that way indefinitely, unless they suffer a huge shock in their lives like when John got shot. I would honestly say that the majority of homeless people have mental problems and many are self medicating with drugs and alcohol.

There is an older homeless couple that spends the night at our house once in a while. They both have a decent income. John and I have been looking for one or two homeless people with an income to share an apartment with us. We figured with their income and our income we could share a decent apartment and we could all save money. They made some excuse as to why they couldn't. They said they were getting their own place. A few months after that, we noticed that they were still homeless. We approached them about sharing an apartment again. And, again, they said no.

John and I haven't been addicts in years, but we still recognize all of the signs. They are doing what John and I used to do. They know that if they pay a full amount of rent that it will cut into their drug money. They also know that they won't be able to do that in our house.

I remember those days. I wouldn't go back there for anything. In means the world to me to be able to cook in and clean my own house. God is so good!

49 THEY WAY JOHN IS

Most of the time, when we are at the library, I am writing or on the computer. John gets on the computer, too, but he spends most of his time mingling with our homeless friends.

Due to the gunshot, John had a stroke. His short-term memory is not that good. You can tell him something one minute, and he'll forget the next.

It's the darndest thing! I was watching John as he was talking with the homeless people. He was able to recall previous conversations with every person. I'm talking about details. He asked questions. He offered guidance. That wasn't new. John always shares an encouraging word for someone.

For John, God is most important. So, he says, "God bless you," to everyone who passes us. He wants the best for everyone. He has tried to help friends, family, and strangers alike. Most people fail to use his help for what it was intended. They take his kindness for weakness. They try to get all they can from him and they never pay him back. We don't really look for it back. God takes care of us.

It's just disappointing to see how the same people we were on the streets with now set out to use us. We still love and pray for them. We never hold a grudge.

God bless them all.

50 THE LONG-TIMERS

We came to the library to get on the computer. We never made it past the tables outside. There was a small group of "long-timers" sitting at the table. I had come to say, "Hi" to everyone. Before I knew it I was sitting down.

We were sitting there talking and laughing. We were reminiscing about the past. We've got so many memories of being homeless.

I was sitting there feeling bad for everyone. They've been out here for so long. Every last one of them has had a place to stay over the years, but they always lose it. I know that they are tired and hungry. They are resigned to living this difficult life. They have no hope.

We wish to help everyone, and have tried. John and I have learned that we can't save everyone. It's sad, but true.

51 MY CROSS

We were on the streets many years ago, before John got shot. St. Ben's had a women's day for the homeless women. There was a very nice woman in charge. There were snacks and many activities. They even gave us massages. The volunteers were kind and attentive. They really seemed to want to make our day special. Our first book was but a manuscript in progress. I showed it to the lady in charge. She liked what she read and bought a copy from us.

Several long tables were set out with purses, costume jewelry, and make up from Boston Store. Everything was beautiful. These were things we would all love to have, but could never afford. These were the prizes we would pick from when we got bingo. We were all excited.

Bingo started, so I hurried to sit down. We played bingo, but it wasn't traditional bingo. Today all of the numbers were called, so everyone was a winner. So many things had been donated by the Boston Store that we all won twice. I didn't know what to pick. When I won my first bingo I went up to the tables. As soon as I stepped up to the tables, my eyes were drawn to a cross on a black string. I knew I had to have it. I thought I had already seen everything, but I know I hadn't seen this. Almost everyone on the trail wears some sort of cross. I knew this one was special. The second time I got bingo I picked out a cute purse. That was six or seven years ago. That cute purse is long forgotten, but I continue to wear that cross every day. I was wearing that cross when John was shot, and I wore that cross the entire year he was in the hospital. I wore that cross until the black string wore out. Then, we put it on a chain. After that, we bought a chain for it that won't change color. That cross will always be special to me. Recently, John put a dainty chain and cross on lay away for me. It is really beautiful. At first, I felt like I was betraying the cross that I've worn on the streets all of these years. I had to tell myself that as long as I remember my cross, and what it represents to me, it would be okay to wear a new one.

Thank you, God!!

52 NOWHERE TO GO

The sign had been posted for quite a while. The library would be closed for the holiday. The library is a place where the homeless stay in all day out of the weather. When the holidays come, the library closes. And, if the library is closed, almost everything else is closed. Where are the homeless supposed to go to stay warm? Most of the time they spend the holiday outside.

John and I knew that the library was closed for the day. On Mondays the museum is free for Milwaukee residents, so we decided to go there. We got ready to go. We drove down by the museum. It's across the street from the library, so that's where we parked. We walked to the museum.

We went into the museum to get our free admission bracelets. There is a sun room with tables and chairs. We used to hang out there when we were homeless. That's where I wrote a lot of the first book. The people who work at the museum knew that I was homeless back then. One of the workers told me that they didn't mind that homeless sit there under two conditions: first, they have to stay out of trouble, and second, they have to move to a table in the other room when the school kids come there for a field trip. They said we could go back in the sun room when the students left. I thought she was nice and that the museum had a refreshing attitude when it came to the homeless.

Today, when we walked into the museum, I could see that things haven't changed. There were about thirty homeless people sitting in the sun room. They had been there for several hours.

They still had plenty of time left to sit there before St. Ben's started serving. They passed time in various ways. Some were reading. A few people were playing dominoes. Other people were talking. The scene took me back. This was definitely an important place for past homeless like us and will hopefully still be a place of refuge for future homeless. A few homeless people will mess it up for the majority. You wouldn't believe where you'll sometimes find a brief moment of peace on the streets.

Thank you, God!

53 A SINGLE WOMAN

There is a lady who we see downtown who always seems to be drunk every time we see her. She is a sweet woman. She always greets John and me with a loving hug. She hugged me like that the first day I met her. We haven't known her very long and she's not downtown every day. I'm not sure if she's homeless or not. We just don't see her enough to know if she has a home. She doesn't carry a back pack or any bags with her.

Tonight, when we left the library, she was outside crying. I tried to understand her when she was talking to me. It was difficult with her being drunk and crying. I did understand her when she asked for a ride somewhere. I asked her if it was a safe place to stay for the night. She said it was. She got in the back seat.

John and I were having a disagreement about something. She piped in with, "You should just love each other." Then, she asked us to change the radio station. John did it for her. We were discussing our problem again when she told us to give each other a hug. We were not in the mood yet to hug. Besides, I was driving. In her inebriated mind she was trying to help us. Like I said before, she is a sweet lady.

We arrived where she told us to take her. She got out, but hesitated to walk away from the car. I felt bad for her. I wanted to take her home with us for the night. We already have someone staying with us. We really have no more room.

She was mumbling incoherently. Then, she said something to me that really made me worry. She told me, "If something happens to me, my last name is_____." She told me her last name. I had a hard time understanding what she said. With that she walked away from the car.

When we got home we found her purse in the back seat. I put it up for her. I'll give it back to her when I see her again. In the meantime, I would like to ask God to keep her warm, fed, and safe.

I saw her a few days later and I gave her back her purse. She told me she was drinking. That was nothing new. She's always tipsy when I see her. That was quite a few months ago.

54 WHAT WOULD YOU DO?

What would you do if you unexpectedly lost your source of income? It could happen. Are you prepared? What would you do if you found yourself on the streets with no money? What would you do if you had no family or friends to turn to? That's how it is for many homeless people. What would you do if you had to sleep outside? Do you even know where to sleep? Do you have blankets? Do you know where to get them?

How would you find another job? You don't have a cell phone to use. Do you know where to make phone calls and where to receive messages? If you find a job how do you keep it? Do you get to shower regularly? Do you know where you can go to use a shower? How would you deal with the police harassing you at night? Some nights they follow you from spot to spot, making you move around all night. Where do you turn to for legal help when you are homeless? How would you know how to find help with all of your questions? Is there help for someone like you?

Could you swallow your pride and learn to be humble? You have to when you are homeless. Could you bear the looks that strangers will give you? Could you learn to start over? When you become homeless you have start from the bottom. You have to start from scratch. Could you be strong? You have to be strong to endure the streets. Not everyone can make it out here.

Could you survive on the streets? Only God knows…

55 ANOTHER TRIP TO THE LINE

The weatherman was right today! It is frigid outside! This is the time of year when we lose the most homeless. I touch on this subject a lot because people are dying needlessly. John and I went to the library, as usual. We got on the computer for a little while. We decided to go home. On our way around the side of the library, we see a familiar little bus. This lovely church brings hot soup, hot cider, sandwiches, etc. I've talked about them before.

They set up tables on the sidewalk to serve off of. I asked the lady where her gloves and hat were. She wore none. I could tell that she was freezing in her small coat. She was dressed as if she were riding in the car. Not only did the volunteers freeze while they were serving us, we froze while waiting in line for our food. It took me back. We have to stand in line and eat our food out in the elements. There is no sitting down at a table. We stand up and eat our food in the sun, rain, wind, and snow. People walk by the line of people and the little bus and they stare at us.

Could you imagine the feeling?

Can you really?

56 BOARDERS

I've talked about our boarders before. We often take one or two homeless people home with us. We can get in trouble and could get kicked out of our place for doing this. We keep reaching out to people anyway. We'll see someone who is struggling, or just someone who needs some rest, and we'll take them home for a couple of days. We can't seem to help ourselves.

In the past, we have tried taking in a homeless person with an income to share the apartment. We split the bills. It helps us all save a few dollars. It would be an ideal situation. We can't seem to find a homeless person with an income who really wants to settle down, though. Take the following person, for example. This person has already lived with us twice. He gets a monthly check, but, more importantly, John has a soft spot for him. He sincerely cares about this man. I'm more skeptical. He has already messed up with us before. I'll tell you about that in a minute.

At this point, we have taken in forty to fifty people in a four year span. We want our house to be a safe place where a person can start over. I've already talked about how we treat people when they are in our home. All of the basics are provided to become a success. With an address and a phone it is much easier to find a job.

John always helps people out with whatever money they need throughout the month. It's only a little at a time, but it all adds up. All he asks is that they pay him back. That's how this person ended up owing John some money. We were getting ready to move. We told him how much the rent would be at the new place. He said, "Okay."

When this guy gets his check he likes to gamble. We would go to the casino with him to get our money, or we wouldn't get it. He went to pick up his food stamp card at his former address and he didn't come home for three days. When he got back he lied to us about where his food stamps went. So, for the whole month he borrows money and eats our food. Every time we cooked we included him. He ate a lot, too.

We thought he was going to move to our new house with us, but he disappeared a few days before he got his check. Not only did he not clean up behind himself before he left, he didn't tell anyone he was leaving. He just disappeared. That was the same thing he did before.

We gave up. Nobody wants the help that we are trying to offer. All of these people stayed at our house and not one person got themselves together. It was so discouraging. We decided to just get our house by ourselves. It sounded good.

Well, we did have one more friend who wanted to stay with us. We were skeptical after all of these failures, but we decided to give him a chance. So much for having our own place!

Everyone talks a good game when they move in, but the proof is in the pudding. Time always tells the truth. Like I said before, people start off in a positive mode, and then they fall off.

The friend we decided to help this time started off way better than the rest. It was the day after check day and he still had his whole check. He helped us move to the new place. He went to the furniture store and Wal-Mart with us and bought his own bed and television for his bedroom. The next day he bought himself several pairs of shoes. Nobody else has ever done that.

We were very impressed. People always count on us to provide everything for them. So far this young man seems to be pulling his weight. I'll let you know how it goes.

Only time will tell.

57 ANOTHER BOARDER STORY

In the last story we decided to only take in one boarder. Things can change in one week. We know a couple who is sleeping outside. We had been trying to get them to be our roommates for the longest time. They both have income, but they were dragging their feet to commit to sharing a place with us. They do like John and I used to do. We would get a motel room and use it to get drunk and high for about a week. The rest of the month is spent sleeping outside. The problem is that the wind chill is below zero. They have come out of a motel to a freezing cold winter. He is up in age, a senior citizen. She's tiny. They can't survive sleeping outside.

Although it's going to be a little crowded, we have to take them in. We want to help everyone, but God only has us help a few at a time.

I guess that's the way He wants it

58 SHE'S ADDICTED TO THE STREETS

This is a continuation of the last two stories...

He came up to us and said, "If you guys can take my girl home with you, I can fend for myself. She almost froze to death Monday night." We said, "Yes," immediately.

For this story I will refer to her as "E". We took "E" home with us. We all ate a home-cooked meal. Later we had snacks and watched movies. I told her that I had clean towels if she wanted to take a shower. Her hair was dirty. I know she needed a shower. She said no. she told us that someone had stolen all of her clothes. She didn't want to put dirty clothes on after taking a shower. She said she would make an appointment at an area clothing bank the next day.

When we got up I made everyone a big breakfast. John and I had errands to run. She wanted to be dropped off at the library so she could see her boyfriend of three years, "M." We dropped her off and left. We came back a few hours later. She had made no effort to get herself some clothes. She was getting drunk on the bus stop with a man besides her boyfriend.

All together she spent two nights with us. The third day "E" and "M" broke up. She called to tell us she'd be gone for the night. John and I were surprised that she left so soon. We thought she was enjoying herself. She was in a hurry to get back on the trail.

We were also surprised that she chose the trail over a nice warm place to sleep. She's addicted to the streets. She didn't want to get herself together. Since then she's been with a different man

133

every time we see her. It's like losing a three year relationship didn't even affect her.

Since "E" didn't want to stay with us "M" moved in. Since he's been with us we've included him in every meal. When his food stamps came due he sold them. He didn't offer to contribute a dime towards any food for the house. We had to tell him that he is responsible for feeding himself. We will still include him in some meals, but, for the most part, he's on his own. Everyone in our house contributes. We all eat together. If you don't want to chip in with everyone else you are on your own.

I don't know if everyone sets out to use us or it just happens that way. At times we feel so disappointed after trying so hard to help someone who doesn't want to be helped. We just want to thank God for these opportunities to be a blessing to someone else.

59 CHRISTMAS

On Christmas Eve, John and I ran to the store to get some last minute sides for our Christmas dinner. We had "M" with us. We already had a turkey and most of the sides, so we didn't have to get much. "M" helped us locate the items we needed.

When we got home, John and I started cooking. We wanted everything ready for Christmas. We seasoned and stuffed the turkey. We picked and washed the greens. We put them on to boil. I made potato salad. John made pinto beans with bacon. We baked two cakes and a cherry cheesecake. We left the cornbread and canned yams for the next day. They would be easy to make. It took us most of the afternoon to prepare everything. We recently moved into a decent little house and this is our first Christmas here. We also had two homeless friends with us. One was "M" and the other was our boarder "Y". We wanted Christmas to be a day of family for them as well as ourselves.

In a previous story I mentioned that "E" and "M" broke up. Ever since "E" left, "M" has been staying with us.

"E" has been dating various men after recently ending a three year relationship with "M". I was kind of surprised that she started dating so soon. It was as if the break up meant nothing to her.

Christmas dinner was delicious. John got so full that he didn't want to take his mom home. We just wanted to go to sleep. We all enjoyed ourselves.

We just want to thank God for the beautiful Christmas and family atmosphere.

60 THE DAY BEFORE NEW YEAR'S EVE

It was the day before New Year's Eve. We had two homeless friends staying with us for a couple of days. We'll call them "W" and "C". The weatherman predicted sub-zero temperatures and several inches of snow, so we had them spend a few days. This is also including "M" and "Y". "M" came to us and said, "E" is sleeping outside. She'll die in this weather." We picked up "E" two days before New Year's Eve.

"E" had been seeing various men. Some had been slapping her around. She drinks a lot and sometimes she flips out. She has mental issues that she refuses to take medication for, because she will have to stop drinking. She's not a bad person. She has issues like everyone else. After she left our house the first time, she managed to secure herself a room in a rooming house. She hadn't got her check yet, but the landlord was willing to hold her debit card until she got her money. That only lasted a few days. She got drunk and flipped out. The guy that she was seeing at the time slapped her. The landlord kicked them out immediately. Now she was back at our house.

Out of seven of us, six receive a check on the first of the month. On the day before New Year's Eve, everyone that gets a check received their small checks. What I mean by that is we receive a small check of eighty dollars along with our regular check every month. Eighty dollars is not enough to do much with, but it was enough for everyone to buy their cigarettes and beer. John and I don't drink, but we allowed them to drink on the condition that everyone remains respectful of the house and each other. We had no problems with anyone. They watched movies and talked. There was a lot of laughter. Every once in a while "E" would stumble and fall down. She is very small, so she got drunk fast. Every time she fell, she would stay there for awhile. We were all laughing. As I listened to them from the other room, I was grateful. We can't save everyone, but at least these five people were safe right now.

Everyone got their regular check on New Year's Eve instead of on the first due to the holiday. We had told everyone that January was the coldest month of the year. We let them know that they could chip in on the bills and stay with us for the month. They would have had to pay little or nothing. They would have most of their checks left to do what they wanted. "E" and "M" got back together.

We all woke up early on New Year's Eve. Everyone had their own plans. John and I wanted to make sure that everyone got to where they wanted to go. We only have so much room in our car, so we had to make a couple of trips. The first people we dropped off were "E" and "M". They wanted to go to the motel for a week so they could get drunk and high, like they do every month. I don't know what they are going to do for the last three weeks of January. We then picked up "W" and "C". They fared better than "E" and "M". We took "W" and "C" to pick up their money. Then, we took them to their campsite to pick up their clothes and blankets. After that, we took them to a rooming house where they paid the rent for the month. This is a furnished room that they can afford. We don't have to worry about them anymore. Our boarder, "Y", opted to continue living here.

Everyone spent a few days with us. The house was full. Then, they went their separate ways. We send our love and prayers with each one of them.

61 DEEP FREEZE

Yesterday, as John and I prayed over our breakfast, I had tears in my eyes. It is thirty-five below zero with the wind chill. All we could think about was how many people and animals were living outside suffering. We prayed to God to keep everyone safe. We also prayed a prayer of thanks. We have a roof over our heads. We have plenty of food. We have all the amenities of home. We are so thankful. We just keep remembering the days when we were the ones sleeping in the deep freeze. How life changes...

There are overflow shelters open in the winter. There's not enough room for everybody, but it's definitely a blessing. They save many lives every year. Even if there was room for everyone, many would never come. For some, it's a matter of pride. They don't want to follow someone else's rules and regulations. Many are hard core drinkers. They get permanently barred from these shelters and meal sites. I don't understand barring a person in the winter, regardless if how drunk they are. This is life and death. An intoxicated person is more susceptible to the elements than a sober person. Some are couples who would rather stay together outside, than to sleep in separate shelters every night. For some, it is the often super early curfew that turns them off. Many may have had a negative experience while staying at a shelter. The list goes on...

At this point of the story we ask you for prayers, time, donations, money, and volunteering to help those less fortunate. This has to happen every day; not just on holidays.

Thank you and God bless you all!

62 THEY'RE BACK...

We knew that they were going to ask if they could come back. Their time was up at the motel. Their money has been long gone. The party was over. Like we have told "E" and "M" before they left, January is the coldest month of the year. We knew that they were making the same bad decisions that John and I used to make over and over. It is a decision that could prove fatal. They didn't think about what they were going to do after their time was up at the motel. Temperatures have already gone to thirty-five below zero. There have been quite a few days that have been below zero so far.

It's so hard to make people listen to you. They are stuck in their ways. They continue to make the same mistakes over and over. I start to get frustrated, but then I have to remember that we used to be the same way. We didn't want to hear what people were trying to tell us, either. We wanted to do what we wanted to do.

So, "M" calls us and asks us if they can stay with us for ten days. We told them yes. They got here last night. We bought a futon since the last time they were here. We bought it because it turns into a bed. They had been drinking, so they slept really well.

This morning we all got up. We let them know that if they were going to sleep on the futon, they have to shower regularly. They obliged by each taking a shower. Nobody ate breakfast. John was making lunch. "E" and "M" have no money or food stamps left. We knew it was too cold to walk to a meal site. John made them something to eat. They were hungry.

The next ten days will prove interesting. I'm sure they will provide us with a couple more stories. We love them dearly. We can't change them. We can only pray for them and be there for them when they need us. At some point most would eventually give up on them.

At what point is it alright to give up on anybody?

63 THE STORY CONTINUES

We are half way through the ten days that "E" and "M" want to stay with us. They agreed to chip in a few dollars on the bills. When "M" gets his check, they will probably leave overnight. He doesn't receive a whole lot of money on his check, so they won't be gone longer than that. They know they can't use those drugs in our house. After that they will come back here until the first of the month. We don't condone those using hard drugs, but we don't hold it against them. John and I come from the same place in addiction that they are in now. Drugs were very important to us; too important to pay the rent somewhere. We just ask that they don't steal from us.

We are hoping that if they spend enough time in the comfort of our home, maybe they'll want the same for themselves. We've seen many people who have left our house and then acquired their own place to live. In most instances, they end up losing it eventually (usually because they are taking too many other homeless people to stay in their apartment), but many times they were able to get another place to live.

"E" and "M" haven't been drinking much. They don't have the money. John took pity on them and bought them some beer. It wasn't very much. Nobody got sloppy drunk. I was listening to John, "E", "M", and "Y" in the other room. They were all laughing and having a good time. It's times like these that make all the effort worthwhile. We are blessed to have each other. It's not always fun and games. We argue just like we are a family, but for the most part, we have a great rapport with each other.

John and I believe that this is going to be an ongoing situation with "E" and "M". They are going to need to stay with us between checks every month. At least we know that they are safe for now. That's all we can ask for.

It's in God's hands now...

64 "T"

We met her at the casino. She seems pretty nice. We'll call her "T". She told me that she is homeless. We can identify with that.

"T" stays in the casino for weeks at a time. She may start off with a few dollars of her own. The rest of the time she befriends people gambling at the casino and then tells them that she's homeless. They take pity on her and they give her money. She then runs to her favorite slot machine. She's at the casino for such long stretches that she is exhausted and starving.

When we first met her she told us her story. She has two children who stay with her aunt. "T" told me that she doesn't get along with her aunt. She rarely sees her children. She is too ashamed. "T" was distressed. She told me that she used to have money to buy them toys. Now she doesn't have any money. She also said that she hasn't seen her babies in so long. I could see the guilt all over her face. I told her that her children didn't want toys, they wanted their mom. I told her to stop feeling guilty and go see her kids. She was crying, but she left immediately to go see them.

We've offered to let her spend the night many times, but she always gives some lame excuse as to why she can't spend the night. I didn't know what the reason was at first.

We saw "T" at the casino yesterday. She has been there since Monday and it's Saturday now. She gave me the usual song and dance. She told me that she's been at the casino all week. I don't know if she's eaten lately. That didn't seem to bother her at the moment. "T" told me that security has already woken her up twice.

They told her to get up and walk around to keep awake. They don't want to put her out in below zero weather. They said if she falls asleep again that she will be kicked out of the casino. We asked her again to spend the night at our house. Her response was, "When are you leaving? I don't want to miss this lady. She said she would give me a few dollars if she wins bingo." I knew then that I was going to stop asking her to spend the night. She was more interested in gambling than being in a warm house. She asked us to give her a few dollars. "T" said that if she gambled she would be able to stay awake. We have given her money before. We didn't give it to her this time. I didn't want her to gamble. I wanted her to use the money we give her to get on the bus and go to her aunt's house.

It really seems like she doesn't want to leave the casino. I saw her a little later. Apparently, the woman had given her some money. "T" was playing at the slot machine. I came up behind her. She had enough to get on the bus and go see her kids, but she was gambling. Gambling is the same thing as a potent drug to some people. We feel bad for her. What can we do? We can't force her to stop gambling. It's disheartening to see such a sweet girl going through such a hard time. She refuses our help unless it's some money. She is really addicted to gambling. All we can do is love her and pray for her.

65 "A"

We've been friends with "A" for ten to fifteen years. John and I were homeless at the same time as she was. We all slept outside together. There was a rather large group of us. We are considered to be the "long-timers".

"A" is a nice woman who gets used a lot. She will give everything she has. She struggles with her drinking. She quits for quite a while; only to go back to it later. She has mental issues that she deals with. I'm not sure if she takes any medications for it. Alcohol is a way to self-medicate. She has been off the streets for a couple of years. Although, she's been off the streets for a couple of years, she has remained technically homeless. I say that because she has been living in a motel room with her son who has occasionally kicked her out of the room leaving her no place to go. She often trusts the wrong people. She has been hurt a lot. Yet, she continues to be a sweetheart.

John and I stopped by the motel to see "A" and her son. We started talking to her son about getting a place. He said they were paying almost $300 per week to stay at the motel and the manager is talking about raising the rent again. We told them about our land lord. He is a good guy who makes the repairs on the house when needed. They told me that they had an eviction on their records. Our landlord was willing to give John and me a chance even though we had an eviction on us. He only asked us to be completely honest. So, we asked him if he would be willing to help "A" out. He said that would be no problem. We set up a time to see the house.

The motel where "A" is staying is across the city from our house. We picked up "A" and her daughter-in-law. We drove back across the city so they could see the apartment. It was a nice place. They were very excited. The former tenant left quite a bit of furniture, appliances, and dishes. The landlord asked "A" if she could use any of the stuff that was left. She happily accepted everything. At least they didn't have to start over without furniture, appliances, etc. what a blessing! "A" was honest with the landlord. He told "A" that they could have the apartment.

As we drove back across town to drop them off at the motel, they were talking excitedly about the apartment. They are supposed to move in, but we haven't heard from them in a couple of days. We don't know if they are going to move in.

Update: "A" and her son called to see if we have a television they could borrow. They had moved in! We took them a television and a DVD player.

It felt good to help them get into a better place. God is so awesome!

66 A NEW ROOMMATE

Our boarder, "Y", called us to say that he has a new girlfriend. He said he wanted us to meet her. John told him that we would see him when we got home. "E" and "M" just came back from the motel. They are broke from partying. Now they are with us for the rest of the month. They will probably only be with us for the winter. When it's warm again they will most likely start sleeping outside again. Many homeless people find a place to stay for the winter, only to sleep outside for the rest of the year.

When we got home, everyone was in the kitchen drinking and playing dominoes. "E", "Y", and "M" were there along with "Y"'s new girlfriend. We'll call her "R". I think we have seen her around. We gave each other a hug. She told me that she is homeless.

She seems like a nice enough person. We don't really know her. We don't know what her plans and goals are. We'll just have to see what she's about.

At this point of the story "R" has been with us for a couple of weeks. We have found out that "R" has some extensive mental problems. She takes almost as many psych drugs as I do. When we are calmly correcting her she tends to start crying. She is very emotional. She has a lot of ups and downs. I've told her repeatedly that she doesn't have to cry when we tell her something. I had to let her know that we are not mad at her. We are just letting her know how to do things. She requires a lot of attention. One night

147

she was up at three in the morning trying to play the radio loudly while everyone was asleep. When corrected by "Y" she got highly upset. "R" still seems to be a pretty nice person. She doesn't spend all of her time at home. She gets out of the house a lot to visit friends. So far she seems to be a good person.

I will keep you updated...

I already have an update. "R" came home from her friend's house one day. She immediately started crying when I told her that she needed to follow the house rules and to respect the others who live here. She was having problems getting along with the others. She cries every time we say something to her. After she pulled this so many times I called her on it. I said to her, whether she was truly crying or not, that she has to follow the rules or find somewhere else to go. We didn't want her to leave, but she ended up leaving. We have to have structure and respect with this many people in the house. It's the only way we will be able to function together.

We wish "R" well. We pray that she is safe and happy. God bless you, "R".

67 THE END (FOR NOW)

When I first started writing this book, I was unsure of what to say. I thought that I had said it all in the first book. As it turns out, the subject of homelessness is never ending.

There are countless people living on the streets. Many people stereotype the homeless. We are trying to make it plain that people are homeless for many reasons. It's not always their fault. Much homelessness is due to mental illness. These people need more help than what they are getting. They need complete care to meet all of their needs. We need to do something different to keep these people from becoming habitually homeless.

Our dream is to open up houses for the homeless. At first we considered opening up a building. We decided that that was too impersonal. We'd rather offer a home type environment. To open these houses we need donations and book sales. These people are suffering and/or dying daily. They need our help. Please, consider helping those who need you.

God bless you...

ABOUT THE AUTHOR

Laura Marsh spent many years homeless on the streets of Milwaukee, Wisconsin with her fiancé, John. They now live in an apartment. She hopes these stories about her experiences being homeless and the people she met while living on the streets will help readers better understand, respect, and help the homeless people who live in every community.

Made in the USA
Monee, IL
16 November 2022

17920293R00095